Tha ♡ for ins...
Jude! your
chapter is
16. innerchange-
is throughout
the book
esp.
chapter 8
Since it's

been so
impactful
for me!

♡

GETTING NAKED LATER

GETTING NAKED LATER

A GUIDE FOR THE FULLY CLOTHED

KATE HURLEY

ISBN: 978-1-938633-14-0

Published in association with Samizdat Creative, a division of Samizdat Publishing Group (samizdatgroup.com).

Cover design: Luke Flowers (lukeflowers.com)

Visit the author's website at www.katehurley.com.

Contents

This book is dedicated to my father,
Mark Hurley.
You were a good papa, and I miss you.

Introduction

Do I Really Need a Minivan in the Game of Life?

I was playing cards with my little friend Isabella the other day. We were playing Old Maid.

You know the game. You each have a set of cards. You draw from the other player and lay down the pairs that you find. Twos, twos, twos. There is anticipation every time a card is drawn from the other player's hand. Who will pair up next?

Another pair, and another pair, and another pair. Each laid down, one right next to the other.

There was one card left in my hand at the end of the game. The old maid. The card had a picture an older woman surrounded by cats. Apparently cats are the only creatures that will live with single ladies who are mature in age.

Isabella pointed at me and said, "Look, Kate! You have the old maid! That means you are the loser."

I didn't know what to do with this statement or with this game. I don't usually mind losing games to five-year-olds. But I was a little more sensitive about losing this time. In most games, the last person standing wins. In this game, you lose if you're the last woman standing alone. I'll let you in on the reason this was difficult for me; I am thirty something, and I have never been married. I felt a strange kinship with the old maid. *Am I the loser?* I thought.

I decided to learn more about the history of the game. Here's what I found out: it is a very old Victorian game. There are versions around the world, many with different names. In Brazil, it goes by the flattering name Stink. The English version is called Scabby Queen, a name that brings up even worse images than the picture of the American cat lady. And my personal favorite, the French version is known as Le Pouilleux, which means "the louse." Just in case you don't know what that is, it's a parasitic insect. Another word for louse is cootie. Awesome.[1]

In my research, I also found pictures of some vintage Old Maid games. My favorite was a 1940's deck that had wonderful cartoons of very attractive, curvy women. One woman was riding on an airplane. Another was surfing. A third looked like a successful business lady.

The old maid? A little old single lady, sitting in a rocking chair knitting, which is quite appropriate, since that is where the word "spinster" comes from. One who spins. It seems that single people who are a little older have nothing better to do than to sit in a rocking chair and knit some booties for their favorite nephew.

A few weeks after this incident, I was playing another game with my ten-year-old friend, Collin. The Game Of Life. This game has versions of it dating all the way back to 1860. It has a track on which players move in little plastic cars through various life scenarios. Interestingly, in the late 1980s, the game changed the car from a convertible to a Chrysler-esque minivan.

"Wait a second," I said to Collin. "What if I want a four-wheel drive Subaru instead of a minivan?"

Collin retorted, "You have to have a minivan in The Game of Life."

Well, I realized, it made sense that you would need to have decent leg space in a car, since you have to put your growing family into it.

Your family is acquired toward the beginning of the game, when you hit a stop sign in front of a three-dimensional chapel. It is here that you *must* get married and put a new blue or pink peg beside you in your minivan. I looked at Collin and said, "Hey, what if I don't want to get married? Or what if, by some crazy turn of circumstance, it just doesn't happen for me?"

Collin gave me a quizzical look and said, "You can't do that, Kate! You have to get married in The Game of Life."

It's true. I did. If I didn't, I would be stuck at the beginning of the game. Forever. I gave in, but mostly because you get $5,000 worth of wedding gifts on the next space.

At the end of the game, the bank paid out money for various things. I wasn't at all surprised that you received a decent amount for each child that you were able to raise in your minivan. According to Milton Bradley, apparently, he who dies with the most kids gets the most cash.[2]

These are some of the stereotypes that are placed in our minds at a very young age, and I admit I can relate to some of them. Like the old maid, I have seen my friends pair up two-by-two. I am not as old as she is, but I am in my thirties, which is pretty old to be single, especially in Christian circles. And yes, I do put my knitted creations on Etsy.

But that's where our similarities stop. I don't like cats, I have many other things to do with my time than to sit in a rocking chair, and I am really, honestly, not a loser.

Those are good signs that I am not really an old maid, right?

There are also things in The Game of Life that I can relate to. I often feel like society says to me, You're not married? You don't have children? How could you possibly ride around in your plastic car with one lonely plastic peg in it? Is there something wrong? Are you going to get stuck at the beginning of life and never move on to the rest of your game because of your singleness?

The truth is, I have played a wonderful round of the game of life. I am a songwriter, a worship leader, and a teacher. Since I am typing these words right now, it looks like I am a writer, as well. I've made several albums and have traveled all over the world to sing my songs and teach. More importantly, I have many dear friends who are like family to me.

Despite this, I get very sad when I look at my car with the one pink peg in it. I never really wanted an empty car. But a family has not been a part of my game yet.

This has been on my mind a lot lately, and after talking about the subject to many friends, I realize that it is on a lot of people's minds. There are more single people in the world than ever before. According to the book *Going Solo*, 22 percent of the adult population was single in the United States in 1950. Now, as of 2012, that statistic has risen drastically to 49 percent.[3]

In other words, there are a lot of us. Some have decided that living independently was the best choice for them. Some are divorced. Others, like me, have always wanted to be married but for some reason or another have not been. All of us have probably struggled with feeling rejected a few times. Maybe many times. We have most likely felt the pressure to feel valuable by being chosen by someone. And most likely, at some point in our lives, we have struggled with feeling like a loner.

I am writing this book for all of you. I want you to feel validated. I want you to know that you're not alone. And most of all, I want you to believe that you are deeply valuable. I hope that we can walk down the road toward discovering our value together.

Here is what I don't want to do with this book:

I do not want to say that if you follow this formula, you will get yourself a mate. First of all, if I knew that formula, I would already be married. Second of all, in my experience, God seldom works in formulas.

I do not want to say that the sole answer is to be satisfied in God alone. I believe that it is important to be as deeply connected with the Lord as possible. It is part of the answer. But God loves family, and he understands that our relationship with him is different than a relationship with a flesh-and-blood person.

I do not want to promise that God will give us the

desires of our hearts—at least not in the way that we
expect them to be given to us. Ultimately, he will give us
our desires, even if it's not in this lifetime. But the hard
truth is that there are people out there who long to be
married who never will be. Who want children but won't
have any. There are others who will end up with very
difficult marriages. We will challenge ourselves to believe
in God's goodness even when our perspective says that
he is not listening to our prayers.

I do not want to give you the "contentment sermon."
We will talk about how important it is to be thankful
for where we are in life, but we will also talk about the
need to be honest about our feelings. We will look at the
paradox of being thankful while still being honest about
our frustrations.

Here's what I do want to do with this book:

I want to tell my truth, not just what will sell in a
Christian bookstore.

I want to give hope that is still hope even if it doesn't
end in a wedding dress.

I want married people and the church at large to
have a better understanding of what singles and divorced
people go through so that they can better support us.

I want to look at the unique challenges Christian singles face and to explore some of the unhealthy
perspectives of the Christian culture when it comes to
dating.

I want to search the beautiful heart of God and
discover how he sees us.

I want a wonderful man to read this book, write me
romantic love letters, hug dating hello, and marry me, so

that my next book will be called *Getting Naked in a Couple of Minutes: A Guide for the Scantily Clad.*

Our story begins with an event that traditionally ends the story: a wedding.

Make that thirty-three weddings.

Chapter One

If You Can't Marry 'Em, Write a Book about 'Em

I have been in thirty-three weddings. I am not talking about how many I've been *to*; I'm talking about how many I've been *in*.

I'll tell you some of the most memorable:

When I was twenty-two years old,

I was a bridesmaid at my friend Andie's wedding. A few years earlier, I set her up with her future husband, Scott. Their wedding was picture perfect and traditional. Andie wore a beautiful, white tulle dress with a long train and veil. Her hair was piled up on her head. Scott wore an all-white tuxedo. The couple sang "If You Could See What I

See" into handheld microphones while looking into each other's eyes. The organ played. The wedding vows were exchanged. It was beautiful.

If you watch the VHS tape of their wedding, I am the bridesmaid at the end of the line crying profusely. I'm sure people thought I was crying because it was my best friend getting married and not me. But that was not the reason. I was crying because I was overwhelmed thinking about all the people I loved that were at the wedding. I was thanking God that I had such good friends in my life.

When I was thirty years old,

The wedding I was in was the polar opposite of Andie's wedding. It was my brother Will's wedding. The wedding was at a Rainbow Gathering, which is a gathering of about 20,000 people that meet every summer in the national forest. Hippies, Vietnam vets, gutter punks, Hare Krishnas, and everyone in between come together to create a semi-utopian society for about three weeks. I have ministered at the gathering for years, praying for people, leading worship, and giving out food. The believers that I work with every year have become like family to each other.

One year, I invited Will to come to the Rainbow Gathering. He was a shaman at the time. To make an incredible story short, he had a life-changing encounter with God during the gathering that year. He became a follower of Jesus, and he has been one ever since.

Two years later, he married Marie, a dear friend of mine, at the gathering.

I was the wedding coordinator. Marie said to me, "I don't want to do anything. I just want all of our family to give me a wedding." And that's what happened.

Will and Marie got married under a canopy of flowers and branches that our community made for them. There were bagpipes and Irish flutes and about twenty hand drums. The older couples, who loved my brother and his bride like their own children, gathered around Will and Marie and gave them a blessing. Each blessed Will and Marie with the ability to endure something that that particular couple had gone through together, like the ability to make it through a separation, the ability to laugh together, things like that. It was my all-time favorite moment at a wedding.

There was no aisle to walk down at the end of the wedding, so we all circled around the bride and groom and danced. Will spontaneously took Marie's hand and ran with her around a field of sunflowers—God did a fabulous job with the floral design.

Family and friends made the food, baked two cakes, provided the music, made the flower crowns, and did the decorating—all in the middle of the woods. There was something so unique and special about our extended spiritual family coming together to present Will and Marie with their wedding as a gift. It felt like the way a wedding was supposed to be.

Never mind that they spent something like sixty dollars on the wedding. Never mind that I had to walk my shy, conservative dad past mud wrestling in the woods to get there. Never mind that there was a random hippie that walked right up to the couple in the middle of the ceremony to take pictures. It was still the most beautiful wedding I've ever been to.

When I was thirty-two years old,

Two of my dearest friends and neighbors got married. It was a backyard wedding.

Before it started, I spent some time talking to my friend Shannon. Shannon is one of the spunkiest people I know. She and her husband Daniel have been married twenty years and are still deeply in love. They are big fans of marriage—the friendship, the sex, the overcoming of challenges together, the choosing to love. They talk about these things a lot because they think marriage is such a gift. It's inspiring to see the way they love each other.

This is what Shannon said to me that day, as she gestured toward my curled hair, perfect makeup, and eggplant-colored sleeveless dress that showed off my shoulders: "Kate, you look smoking hot. Too bad it's just wasted."

Most of you who are single are probably shaking your heads and putting this comment in the mental file called Insensitive Things that Married People Say to Single People.

Believe me, that mental file in my own mind is chock-full of comments people have made to me over the years, but this was not one of them. I was not offended by Shannon's remark because I knew she meant it as a compliment. I actually felt flattered.

I knew that what she was really saying was, "What

the heck, Kate? You are beautiful inside and out. I don't understand why you're still single."

People say this to me often. It is kind of a mystery to all of us.

During the wedding, I sang a love song that I had written. At the reception, my married friend Seth said to me, "Kate, in that dress, singing that song, any single guy here would want to dance with you." I was quite flattered.

Thinking about these two comments as I was eating my Chicken a la King, I began to feel confident, brazen even. I was beautiful. Someone would want to dance with me.

I started to anticipate the dancing that was about to begin. I imagined that one of those handsome, single groomsmen would see me across the room and think, *That was the girl who sang her song during the wedding. She fascinates me. I want to dance with her.* He would walk up shyly and ask me. He would gently take my hand, and we would step out onto the dance floor together. Even that would give me butterflies, since no one had touched my hand in a long time. And then we would move together. Two people with different personalities, different weaknesses, different strengths, moving as if we were one. Maybe we would even fall in love.

The time came for the single men to ask the single women to dance. I stood at the edge of the floor in anticipation.

No one asked me to dance.

I wanted to say, "Hey! Single guys! Over here! According to my married friends, this dress makes me look smoking hot! Doesn't anyone want to dance with me?"

Finally, someone did ask me to dance. He was a heavyset, socially awkward man we'll call Joe. He took me out to the dance floor, stood opposite me, and did one of the worst versions of the "white man's dance" that I have ever seen. (This is a technical term, by the way. *The Urban Dictionary* defines it as "the uncoordinated, rhythmless nature in which socially awkward people dance."[4] Exactly.)

Joe, thankfully, left after that first dance. I stood on the sidelines again. I waited for the next song, hoping that it would be falling-in-love worthy.

The next song was anything but romantic. Can you guess what it was? I'll give you one hint: it had nothing to do with wedded bliss and everything to do with an athletic club.

That's right folks, "YMCA."

Up until that day, I never understood why this song was a staple at wedding receptions. But now, with Joe's awkward dancing still lingering in my mind, I stood on the dance floor pondering this phenomenon.

"Hmmm," I thought. "The Hokey Pokey was probably invented so that wallflowers who never learned how to jitterbug could go out there and shake their booties. It gave them permission. It was part of the song: 'You put your backside in, you put your backside out.'"

"YMCA" became the Hokey Pokey of the '80s. If you hadn't learned the incredibly complicated '80s dance that involved hopping up and down, you could at least fling your arms out to spell things.

Look at us! Who says we can't dance? We are so coordinated! We can all spell out the acronym of the Young Men's Christian Association in perfect unison!

Finally, I gathered up my gumption and danced with all the other bad dancers. More accurately, I spelled. If you looked closely, though, you would realize that I wasn't in perfect unison with everyone else, because instead of spelling YMCA, I was spelling WPCD. A secret joke between me and myself: White People Can't Dance. This has been a tradition for me at weddings ever since.

The next song was "Macarena," which was the Hokey Pokey of the '90s. This song has the same concept: a dance that even a person in a wheelchair could do. Again, what does this dance have to do with the sealing of a covenant between two people?

In the songs that followed, I participated in all of the traditional dances performed at caucasian-majority weddings. You know, like the squat, the double-squat-spin-clap-and-point, the clap-point-point-clap-point-point-and-squat, the hip-breaker, the caucasian-clap, the point-to-the-Lord, and the fat-rebel.[5]

Finally, toward the end of the reception, the DJ put on the music I really wanted to dance to, even if it was reminiscent of awkward middle school moments.

But no one asked me. There would be no slow dancing for me. Not even in my smoking hot dress.

I wanted love, and, instead, I got the white man's overbite.

Seriously, God? Seriously?

That night was like a snapshot of my life. At the beginning of the reception, I sat at the table with good friends and ate. I laughed. I loved being in their company. I was thankful.

But then the dancing came and everyone took his

partner to dance. Another pair and another pair and another pair. Twos, twos, twos. I sat at the table and slowly ate my wedding cake, an important activity when you don't want to look like you have nothing to do while everyone else is dancing. I cried in the bathroom stall.

This time, it really was because it was not my wedding.

I don't want my singleness to be hard for me. I want to be satisfied in who I am as a single woman. But when I look at those pairs dancing, no matter how hard I try to fight it, I don't feel smoking hot. I feel alone.

I try to remember that I have a wonderful life, as single lives go. I also try to realize that I have it better than almost any single older woman in any other moment in history had it. If I lived as a single woman in another country or in another time, I would be less worried about being a loser and more worried about being alive. I am blessed to live in a time in which I can work to take care of myself and in which I don't need a husband to survive. I try to appreciate my freedom and independence as a single woman.

And yet, if it were my choice, I believe I would give up some of my independence to understand what it's like to be in covenant with someone, even if it was difficult. To have people in my life who were more than just my spiritual family, but who were my blood family. To have a husband and children who would walk with me on this journey. I know that marriage is not the fairy tale that our culture makes it out to be, but I still want it.

I never expected to be single at this age. I thought I would have a family by now. I have had to rearrange my life accordingly, and that has been very difficult for me.

Even though I have a good life, there seems to be another life—a parallel life, if you will—that I am missing out on. A life in which I have a family.

Part of the problem is that I don't know what that parallel life would really look like. Right now it is just a mystery, a fairy tale. If I were actually there, I would probably have days in which I felt useless. I would be exhausted from taking care of my kids. I would most likely feel like the romance between my husband and I waned at times, which would be difficult. I would have relational challenges that I can't even begin to imagine right now. These are the things that my married friends struggle with every day.

My view of the life of my married friends is probably not realistic, in the same way that their view of my life can be romanticized. All that freedom! All the traveling! I do have a lot of freedom, but that's in part because the nature of covenant is that lines are drawn around the people within it. I have a lot of freedom because I don't have a lot of covenant. I often struggle with feeling like my life means less because I have no children and no family to invest in.

All the while, my married friends could be sitting at home in their own day-to-day lives, wondering if their lives mean anything because they are at home every day, trying to understand how to connect to the people they love. Many of them, I'm sure, are wondering about their own parallel lives—lives that do not involve marriage or children.

As my friend Aaron said to me the other day, "We spend the first half of our lives trying to meet the one we will marry. We spend the second half of our lives trying to connect with that person."

Most of us, single or married, struggle with the same root sadness of feeling lonely. One of our biggest fears is to be alone. A 2005 gallup poll about what people fear the most revealed terrorist attacks, death, nuclear war, and, you guessed it, *being alone.*[6] All of us struggle with it. When it comes down to what we want in life—married or single—we are very much the same. We all want to be known.

One of my favorite bands, Waterdeep, puts it this way in their song, "The Worst Is My Being Alone," about two friends conversing about this topic:

> *"Aaron, have you ever had a burning in your chest*
> *That made you just want to be free?"*
> *It was a warm afternoon when she asked him this,*
> *As they sat on the shore of the sea*
>
> *He said, "Kelly, I don't think*
> *I've ever wanted as much*
> *To be free as I've longed to be known.*
> *And of the things that I hate*
> *As I look at my life,*
> *The worst is my being alone."*[7]

All of us desire three basic things: to be loved for who we are, to feel like we're valuable, and to know that we're not alone. For some mysterious reason, we have a really hard time knowing how to give and receive those things.

And yet we want them. We yearn for them. More than wealth. More than success. More than anything. Like the song suggests, even more than to be free, we want to be seen, understood, and loved. Loved in our strong places; loved in our weak places.

Known.

Where did this desire come from? Is a life that has no intimate witness still known? If we never become part of a traditional family, are we doomed to loneliness, or can we build our own, different family? What do we do when no one asks us to dance? Does God see me alone at my table, eating my wedding cake? Does he care? Does he ever feel the same way? These are some of the questions we will explore in the chapters to come.

FIRST, seek to understand! Then to be understood

First, love. before desiring love. others from others

First, see before being seen

Chapter Two

Kate: The Musical

I am sitting in my backyard in Colorado during the changing of the light, my favorite time of day. I have a laptop in my lap and a cup of tea beside me.

And my mind is on you.

I am thinking about the fact that out of all the words in the world, you have chosen to read mine. I am honored that you would do that, and I want to welcome you into my story as best I can.

It is tempting to start out by giving you advice, by telling you about awkward dating moments, or by exploring a passage of scripture about God's view on singleness. It would certainly be less vulnerable to do it that way.

But I want to do more than that to begin this book. I want you to understand that even though I am the one writing the book and you are the one reading it, we are really not that different at all.

So, for now, pretend that you are sitting in the lawn chair next to me, looking toward the Flatirons rock formations in Boulder, Colorado, sipping on chamomile. I am telling you about the journey I have walked to get to where I am tonight. A path that has brought me to places I did not expect to be. A path that has been full of frustration and questioning, but a path that has also been full of joy and great love.

In that way, it is probably a story very much like yours.

I will start by saying that I want to honor my family while I write, so I won't get into too many details about my childhood. It is enough to tell you that I was a sad little girl and that I had good reasons to be sad. I had to grow up very fast. I can safely say that my first fifteen years were some of the most difficult of my life.

I am a songwriter. My songs often bring glimpses of my journey, so I am going to write out certain lyrics for you throughout this chapter when I feel like that song best expresses what I am trying to say.

I wrote a song years ago contemplating what it would be like to go back to the little girl that I used to be and to have a conversation with her. I would tell her that she is trying so hard. That she is so strong. But she would have a hard time believing those things. She doesn't see herself strong or beautiful. She sees herself as the short-haired girl with funny thrift store clothes who people think is a boy. She sees herself as the one without any friends. She sees herself as a girl who will most likely turn into a woman who will fall into divorce and abuse and all of the things that are a part of her life now.

I would hold her in my arms and tell her how brave

she is. I would tell her that she can't even imagine all of
the beautiful moments awaiting her. That someday, she
will travel the world and be amazed by it. That she will
have family and friends all around her that deeply love
her, something I know she prays for every day. And most
of all, I would tell her that she will someday know the
unconditional love of her Creator, who already loves her
deeply, and that his love will change everything for her.

These are the words of the song that I wrote for that
little girl:

I see a little girl in the back of my mind
See daisies in her hand, she's looking to the sky, she is looking to
the sky
She is sitting on the stairs of her two story house and the pain
that she bears
Leaves no tears left to cry, leaves her no tears left to cry

Where is the reward for the ones that have been torn?
Where is the treasure laid for the ones who've known so much
pain?

Hey little girl let me whisper some hope
There's mercy for you that overflows
Everything's going to be all right
Everything's going to be all right
Hey little girl won't you hear me say
There is love enough to cover your shame
Everything's going to be all right
Everything's going to be all right

And that little girl so small and so scared
Has been near so long I forgot she was there
I forgot that she was there

Somehow the pain that she didn't feel passed on to me
A weight too great to bear
Much too great to bear

Someone is standing near
Who will wash away her tears
Someday when she's been found
Her scars will become a crown[8]

After these difficult years as a young girl and an adolescent, I went to high school. It was there that I met some wonderful believing friends who took me in. I started recognizing how beautiful and hopeful it was to follow Jesus. It was the first time I felt a part of a family. Those were very happy years.

Then I entered college. There is something special about your first college years. It's the only time in your life when you constantly get to consume semi-edible all-you-can-eat-food and live in a small town filled with people your own age, a town in which most people's careers involve finding their identity by getting totally wasted. I knew from high school that you don't really need to get drunk to have ridiculous amounts of fun. You just need to play Chubby Bunny. So that's what I did.

About halfway through my freshman year, I dated my first serious boyfriend. It was wonderful and romantic at first, but soon dating him triggered a deep place of wounding in me and sent me into a serious depression.

Those of you who have been depressed understand me when I say that I felt like I was drowning in my sadness. I knew that Kate—the Kate that I liked and that other people liked—was deep in there somewhere. But I couldn't find her. It was as if she were trapped in a fathomless dark well and she had no clue how to climb out of it.

Up to this point, I mostly had been a Christian for the benefits of Christianity. I had family all around me. I got to date guys who didn't call me mean names and who didn't watch *Beavis and Butthead* all the time. If I said the right thing in Sunday School, people would think I was valuable.

Now, all of that was stripped away. My boyfriend broke up with me, saying that I was not the same person he had started dating nine months before. People who admired me as a strong believer wondered what was wrong with me and where my faith had gone. Even my dear friends who tried hard to be there for me told me that they didn't know how to help me and that I was going to need professional help.

All I had left was God. And I didn't know if that was going to be enough.

I was so overwhelmed with grief at times that all I could do was to go back in the woods behind my apartment and cry out to this God that I couldn't seem to reach. Sometimes I would spend six hours there, crying.

After about a year of this depression, I went on a mission trip in Mexico. There was a little cove next to the ocean where I went when I needed time to cry.

One day, as I lay huddled and weeping by the beach, I said, "Lord, at this point, I don't think I can have a family, a job, a life. I am too sad. I feel like I am going crazy. Are you ever going to make me better?"

As clearly as I have ever heard God speak to me, he said, "Kate, look at the ocean." I looked at it, crashing back

and forth and back and forth like it has since the beginning of time. "As many times as the ocean waves keep
crashing back to the shore, that's how many times I'm
going to heal you. That's how many times I'm going to
restore you. That's how many times I'm going to wash you
clean."

Up to that point, I had been hearing a lot of lies in my
head, and I was believing them. Things like, "You aren't
worth anything," "No one loves you," and "You will never
be happy."

But when I heard that promise from God about the
ocean that night, I believed him.

I started dancing around the beach, singing and crying.
My heart was full of joy for the first time in a long time.

That night was a turning point of that season and,
subsequently, of my entire life. I understood that the God
who created me also cared about every detail of my life.

I had what all humans long for. *I was loved.*

My song "You Are Not Alone" is my reflection on this
deep truth that changed my life.

> *Sometimes you get so weary that you run to forget*
> *You keep yourself so busy anything to cover up that*
> *Sometimes life just don't make sense*
> *And the reason for your running is a longing to be known*
> *By someone who says your life is worth it, someone captured by*
> *your heart*
> *Someone you gave up on long ago*
>
> *But you are not alone*
> *You are not alone*
> *His love is all around*

He holds you even now
You are not alone

He will not leave you orphaned, that's a promise he has made
When others leave you empty and the world has left you broken
Still he will not walk away
So come and lay down all your questions
Lay down your striving to be free
He has loved you since you've breathed and
He will love you for forever
Really what more do you need[9]

The four years that followed my college years run together in a blur. They were restless years. I worked at a daycare on and off. I wrote songs that I never sang for anyone. The words *God, please show me what I'm supposed to do* were written over and over again in my journal. This made sense, because these were my "supposed to" years. I wanted God to hand things to me with a perfect bow on them so I wouldn't have to make decisions.

I dated someone seriously during that season, but I was unsure if I wanted to marry him. I distinctly remember him saying, "Kate, I don't want you to just ask God if you're *supposed* to marry me. I want you to also ask yourself if *you want* to marry me."

I didn't like that question because I didn't know what I wanted. A year later, we broke up. I was devastated.

Soon after that, I moved to Colorado Springs to work with Ben and Robin Pasley, the musicians who started the *Enter the Worship Circle* series, which are acoustic, organic, live, and life-changing CDs. I had the privilege of writing and singing on one of the albums in the series. Ben and Robin mentored me for the next few years, teaching me how to use my music as a means to love people.

I developed my mission statement, which was and is "to paint a accurate picture of a passionate God."

For the next ten years, I traveled as a music missionary. It would take up a whole book to tell you all of the adventures I have had while touring. I will just give you the CliffsNotes version: I have led worship at hippie gatherings where a naked guy spat on the cross and a woman wearing fur stood in front of me yelling, "Praise Mother Earth!" I have sung Christian hard rock songs in which I was required to head bang in front of two thousand people in Thailand. I have played in castles in Germany. I have taught homeless people about music and recorded an album of their songs. I have played shows where it was just me and five other people. I have taught students who rose up to become a new generation of worship leaders in Southern Ireland, a place that practiced little but liturgical worship for centuries. I have sung spontaneous love songs from God over women in rehab recovering from heroine addictions, watching them weep one by one.

It has been a full, incredible ten years.

I had a handful of boyfriends and serious crushes during this season. You will get an idea about these relationships as you read this book, but they were all similar. They basically looked like this: Boy meets girl. Girl really really really likes boy. Boy is pretty sure he likes girl. Girl is very in love but afraid of being abandoned. Boy thinks girl is amazing and cares about her but is unsure if she is "the one." Boy breaks up with girl. Girl is in the depths of despair.

Lather, rinse, repeat.

Somewhere in the middle of this, I was bitten by a tick while ministering in Michigan. I went to the doctor to get tested for Lyme disease, and it came back negative.

For the next ten years, I had all kinds of bizarre health problems. I almost lost my finger to gangrene. I had arthritis all over my body. I often had huge welts showing up daily on my skin. I would spit blood.

And then there was the insomnia. I barely slept through the night. I could go seven, eight days without sleeping day or night. When I did sleep, it was only for about three hours or so, and then I would wait nights before I got another three hours. I often had panic attacks when I would try to sleep. This went on for years. It is one of the most difficult things I have ever gone through. My best friend told me years later that when I would leave her house after laying on her couch all day so I wouldn't have to be alone, she would cry because she thought I might not live very long.

I finally went to a doctor who said that every specialist I had seen before and every test had been wrong. I did, indeed, have Lyme disease.

I believed that God heals. I had seen him do it many times, so I was very confused about why he did not seem to be listening to my prayers for my own healing. I was being tortured by my lack of sleep. I was in pain all the time, and I wanted to be in hot water every second of the day. I was completely exhausted. I felt like I was going crazy.

Where was the God who had been so faithful to me in the past?

As I was lying in bed night after night, begging God

for sleep, having absolutely no idea why the God who loved me would not heal me, I would talk to my soul. I would say, "Soul, this does not make sense right now. But you cannot, you CANNOT let go of believing God's goodness."

One of my favorite passages of scripture, which I memorized during my depression in college, was Psalm 30, which says, "Weeping may remain for a night, but rejoicing comes in the morning [. . .] You turned my wailing into dancing; you removed my sackcloth and clothed me with joy, that my heart may sing to you and not be be silent. Lord my God, I will give you thanks forever" (vs 5, 11-12, NIV).

One morning, when my health was at its worst, when I had no strength to get out of bed, I rolled over to my keyboard. I laid my head down on it because I could not keep it up. I put my fingers on the keys and started playing. God gave me a song based out of Psalm 30, a song to sing to my own soul.

Often I write songs for the people who will listen to the song. But this song was for *me*, to give *me* hope. It's called "Joy Comes in the Morning."

> *Awake oh my soul wipe the sleep from your eyes*
> *Look and see what you missed before*
> *Do not give up hope though you've wept through the night*
> *Your light will break forth like the dawn*
>
> *Joy comes in the morning*
> *Joy comes in the morning*
> *Joy comes in the morning*
>
> *Why are you downcast, put your hope in the Lord*
> *He makes all things beautiful*

Remember how he's rescued you before
Be strong now lift your head

Joy comes in the morning
Joy comes in the morning
Joy comes in the morning[10]

I tried hard to believe the words to that song were true.

This was one of the most difficult seasons of my life to be single. I wanted a companion with me, someone who could care about finding a way for me to get better simply so that I could rest. Someone who could hold me at night and tell me it was going to be OK. I wondered if I could ever have that, if anyone would ever love me enough to take on such a huge burden.

I remember coming home from a doctor's appointment, during which the doctor had let me know how serious my disease was. He told me that I could pass it on to my children. There was a slight chance I could give it to my husband if I didn't get better. I wondered if I should just opt out of having a family then and there. I didn't want my husband or children to have to live through this. The doctor also told me that with Lyme, my symptoms would probably get worse for the rest of my life, that it would be almost impossible to cure it.

I stood in my living room after that appointment, my purse and coat still on, and I suddenly became overwhelmed with the weight of responsibility on my shoulders. I was the only one in my life who could get help for this. I was so sick that I could barely walk into a grocery store, yet I was expected to do the hard work of finding some way to get better. I had no insurance and probably could not get insurance with the record I now had. I couldn't work, and the government would not give me disability as Lyme is not a very recognized disease. It was terrifying. I felt utterly alone.

The Alcoholics Anonymous *Big Book* says, "When we were faced with a crisis that we could no longer postpone or evade we had to fearlessly face the proposition that either God is everything or else he is nothing. Choose."[11]

It was time for me to choose. Was God everything to me or nothing to me?

That night I had a dream. I was riding up an elevator and the doors opened. I was in a hospital. A middle-aged man who was slightly overweight with the kindest face I had ever seen came up and gave me a big bear hug. I had the distinct impression that we had started out as pen pals, and over the years we had become very close. He was so happy to see me.

I said, "How is she doing?"

He replied, "She is not well." He had so much concern in his face. I could tell that he loved her with a very pure love.

It was then that I realized that the "she" we were talking about was me. The sick version of me. Suddenly, I was the sick me, in my hospital bed. I was in and out of a coma, and I was very, very sick.

Every single time I woke up, this man was there. Reading to me, doing crossword puzzles, holding my hand. Sometimes I would wake up and he would be eating in the room. He never left my side. Most of the time, I was too sick to say anything. I would just look and see him there and know that I wasn't alone. Then I would fall back into another coma.

Sometimes, he would pick me up and put me into my wheelchair. There was a huge outdoor garden on my floor in the hospital, and he would bring me to look at all the beautiful plants and flowers. He would touch them tenderly and tell me their names and about how they grew. He would take my weak hands and bring them up to the flowers. First, a stunning red amaryllis, then a delicate white orchid, then a big purple iris. I could feel the softness of the petals on my fingers.

He would take me back to my room, lift me out of my wheelchair and into my bed, and I would fall back to sleep as he knelt there, praying.

When I woke up from the dream I realized that the man was not a future husband or a father or a friend. It was Jesus.

Our God has many facets. Sometimes he is riding on a horse with stars in his right hand and a sword coming from his mouth, his face shining like the sun. Sometimes, he is a middle-aged, kind man who reads to us when we are in the hospital. He is the one who kneels down and prays for us by our sick bed. He is the one who does not leave our sides.

This dream helped me to remember that I was everything to him and that made my choice simple: he would be everything to me.

I realized that even though I felt alone, I was never really alone at all.

Soon after this, God led me to a brilliant naturopathic doctor named Dr. Shauna Young, who I now credit with saving my life, or at least with saving me from a very difficult life of chronic illness.[12]

I was officially free of Lyme disease in June 2009, seven years to the day after I was bitten by the tick.

I have absolutely no arthritis any more, no pain. I have energy. I am finally sleeping through the night most nights, now that my brain has had a few years to heal.

I try to thank God every day for my health now. I am so grateful.

In the years that followed my getting better, I went through another depression after a breakup with my boyfriend of two and a half years. I have mourned getting older and not having a family. But one thing I have learned through my journey is this:

God has rescued me before. He will rescue me again.

I am in a mostly happy season right now. I am healthy. I have the most beautiful community surrounding me to walk life with. I am getting to do things that I love to do. I still want a family very much, but I am learning day-by-day to trust God with that.

Song of Solomon 8:5, says, "Who is this coming up from the wilderness, leaning on her beloved?" (ESV).

That verse perfectly describes the journey that I am walking through now. I am coming up out of the wilderness leaning on my beloved. There are a lot of things I don't understand in my life, especially being single. But I do know that I can lean on Jesus. I know that he is trustworthy. And I know that I will never walk alone, no matter what wilderness or mountaintops await me.

How To Make Decisions

1.) Figure out your truth. Not anyone else's. Yours.
2.) Ask yourself, "What would I do if I weren't afraid?"
3.) Do the next right thing.

Chapter Three

The Rant Chapter

I have tried to live life with everything in balance. Having everything in balance will be a theme throughout this book. Favoring one side of the scale all the time will bring chaos. Yin and yang—the harmony of things—is a healthy way to live.

Yin Yin—the imbalance of things—is not a healthy way to live. It is the name of a panda bear.

I promise to bring balance soon. I will discuss in later chapters the wisdom of having realistic expectations of marriage, of being thankful, of looking to God for solace and stability and comfort. You know, all of the things you expect to hear in a book about being single.

But first I need to validate every person who is single who is reading this book. I think we all need to feel understood, even if just for a little while.

I originally thought about calling this book *Pissed Like Hip-Hop: Why Christian Singles over Thirty Have Every Right to be Pissed*. This would be an intentional rip off of the brilliantly written *Blue Like Jazz*, partially because *Blue Like Jazz* is a great title, and partially because that guy made a lot of money off the book and is single and might be flattered.

I chose not to call this book *Pissed Like Hip-Hop* because I didn't want to sound like a bitter and mean single person. I will attempt to sound wise and wonderful for most of this book. But during this one itsy-bitsy chapter, I am asking your permission to sound a little bitter and mean. If you don't like ranting, skip to the next chapter.

Because at the risk of sounding like I am ranting, I am going to rant.

Here goes. Let these words resonate in all of their pity-party glory. Let this sentence be as naked as I want to be someday.

Being single sucks.

There it is, folks. The sentiment almost every single person has thought many, many times—especially those of us who are over thirty. For decades, it has not been socially acceptable in the Christian world to articulate that sentiment without feeling like children throwing a temper tantrum about our love lives.

And yet, I just said it. I should get a Dove award or something.

I am being very honest when I say that I had a hard time writing that sentence. It makes me sound unspiritual, ungrateful, and untrusting. In fact, I have been thinking about rewriting it many times since I typed it.

I read a good book this week, one that I wouldn't have

had time for if I had a family, so I pondered changing the sentence to "*Sometimes* being single sucks."

I babysat five kids today, and I was as frazzled as a one-legged Riverdancer. I thought about adding, "but having a family is difficult, too."

Finally, though, I decided to leave it like it is, for all of our sakes. Nothing softening the blow, nothing added to the end of the sentence. Why?

Because someone needs to say it. That's why.

Something seems to have thrown me over the edge. Maybe it is that website that I was on this morning. When suggesting a password question, it gave me "The date you and your spouse met" or "The name of a bridesmaid in your wedding" or "Your first child's birthday." I inevitably had to choose "The name of your first cat." Even if Samone was the best cat in the world, she was still a friggin' cat.

Maybe it's that when I see a couple kiss, even just in passing, it makes my heart ache a little bit. It makes me think that if I were ever to have that again, I would try to appreciate even the briefest moment of us expressing that we have chosen each other, that we are closer to each other than we are to anyone else in the world.

Maybe it's that I have no idea what to put on my phone's screen saver. I guess a mountain or something.

Maybe it's that I spend about 70 percent of an average day alone. I have spent years like this. Sometimes, it can get unbearably lonely.

Maybe it's that I often feel like I have been perpetually living the life of a college student, roommates and all, for the last fifteen years. I don't even want to think about how many times I've moved during that time.

Maybe it's that I often avoid spending time with my friends' children because I end up wanting to cry almost the entire time.

Maybe it's the story I heard recently about my friend's Bible study, during which an older single woman started crying and talking about her struggles with feeling lonely. A married member of the group scoffingly said, "Why don't you take my kids for a day and I'll go get my nails done."

Maybe it's that I really hate small talk and I really hate getting my hopes up and I really hate hurting people, so I would rather have my teeth drilled than go on eHarmony first dates. I know, I know, all you married people! Online dating is the ultimate answer to my singleness woes! I know that there are a hundred men waiting for me in the online dating world! But ninety-nine of those men are showing off their beer bellies with their shirts off (I am serious, I have had that match), or they leave me messages like, "I have already married and divorced you in my mind," or most commonly, they don't love God like I do. I have to go through a lot of awkwardness and pain to possibly, maybe, find the one out of the ninety-nine. I know that sometimes you need to have a root canal to get a new tooth, so I am giving it a try. But that doesn't mean I have to like it.

Maybe it is that while doing research for this book, I found countless articles with titles like, "Marriage Does not Solve Your Problems," or "How to Stop Postponing Your Life," but none called something like, "Why Singleness Sucks."

Take this quote, for example, from one of the above

articles: "Marriage is about finding a comrade, not ultimate contentment. It's about finding a helpmate, not a healer."[13] I read countless sentiments like this in my research. Here's the thing: I don't think that I have postponed my life. I have tried to live life fully with the hand I have been given. And I am not looking for ultimate contentment or for a healer. I know that contentment is something that I have to work out between myself and God and that I shouldn't project it onto another person. I already have a healer, and I realize that. But I *am* longing for a comrade, a lifelong companion, a helpmate, and it hurts that I don't have one yet. Is there something wrong with that? Are my feelings not valid?

One of the only articles I found that did talk about the difficulty of being single was called "My Secret Grief: Over Thirty Five, Single, and Childless" by Melanie Notkin. In it, the author says, "This type of grief, grief that is not accepted or that is silent, is referred to as *disenfranchised grief.* It's the grief you don't feel allowed to mourn, because your loss isn't clear or understood. You didn't lose a sibling or a spouse or a parent. But losses that others don't recognize can be as powerful as the kind that is socially acceptable."[14]

This sadness, this disenfranchised grief, is what I feel on a semi-regular basis. I have not lost a marriage, but I have never had a lover. I have not lost a baby, but I have never had a child.

It's a strange kind of grief, because people don't often understand it as a loss. It is not socially accepted as a loss. There is not a lot of empathy for it.

It's a different kind of bereavement because it is painful

in a slow, seeping kind of way. It's a dull loss that I am reminded of many times a day. With each reminder, it aches a little bit and adds to the larger ache inside of me. Every day I have to consciously choose to find joy despite these reminders, and sometimes that can be exhausting.

There are funny ways that church culture reflects most people's unawareness of our disenfranchised loss—not in what they *do* give us, but in what they *don't* give us. The sermons that *aren't* given, the prayers that *aren't* offered, the books that *aren't* written. As if what we are going through is not that important.

I remember going to a church service where a pastor tearfully prayed for people in different predicaments: "Lord, I pray for the married people who are struggling through the difficulties of relationship right now. For the divorced people who are wrestling with rejection. And for the single people who (cue a bit of chuckling) don't know how good they have it."

Pastors are almost never single, so they don't often teach on singleness. It is not the particular struggle they are going through, and they often overlook it. I have heard people say that it wouldn't be fair for a pastor to preach on singleness because so many of the members of the congregation wouldn't be able to relate. But, as I stated in a previous chapter, most churches likely have just under half a congregation that is single. We singles have listened to countless sermons on marriage. We have often tried to learn from sermons about family and marriage, even though we can't completely relate to them. It would be nice to have married people give us the same consideration at times.

Similarly, there are thousands of books, even just in the Christian genre, about being married. But there are only a handful about being single. The ones that are about singleness are often about getting a mate or being content with the *gift* of singleness.

I mentioned this to a well-meaning married friend the other day, and she said, "Of course there are thousands of books on marriage! It just shows you how *difficult* it is to be married. All of those books on marriage are needed since it's so hard."

The "marriage is so hard" speech is one of the most popular speeches given to single people, right up there with the "if you just let go" speech, which I will discuss later.

I wanted to say to my friend, "Oh yes, it is a *breeze* to wake up every morning wondering if you will ever be chosen, if you will ever be intimate with anyone, if you will ever have children. These are things that even people in the Bible mourned over! It's really quite easy to think that I might not ever have anyone call me Mom. That if I don't get married, I will always wonder where to go for Christmas because I don't have my own husband and kids to celebrate with. I have no qualms with the haunting thought that if I am still single as an older woman, I will not have a husband or children to take care of me, or even to talk to. That's all really easy. No wonder there are so few books out there about it."

OK. I think I am mostly done now. Thank you for letting me rant; it felt really good. I will talk in my "nice Kate" voice again.

Let me emphasize that I didn't just go on that rant

for the sake of being angry. I simply wanted to take the opportunity to say that singles want so much to be *seen*.

There have been occasions in meetings I have gone to when teachers have validated singles, and their words felt like water to my soul. I remember the time that one of my spiritual papas, Chuck Parry, had all the couples in church stand in a circle. Then, he had the single men stand in a circle inside of the larger circle. Then, he had the single women stand inside of the men's circle. He said, "This is the kind of family we need to be. We need to remember and protect our daughters." That meant the world to me.

Last week I went to a conference hosted by Inner-CHANGE, an organization that sends teams of missionaries to move into poor neighborhoods around the world in order to love them well. The conference featured a panel to discuss the topic of families, and, shockingly, there were several single people on the panel. The entire panel spent the majority of the time talking about the single people on their teams and how the other team members could bless these singles and be family to them since the singles didn't have a traditional family of their own. The panel discussed how married people should never reduce singles to live-in babysitters. They talked about how the singles should be able to speak into the lives of the married people on the team, that they should never be considered lower on the totem pole because of their married status, and that singles should be able to be leaders over the married people if that was the best fit.

The couples asked the single people on the panel how the married people on their teams could benefit them and help them through the challenges of being single. I was so honored that they noticed people like me, that they remembered us, and that they validated our relational challenges, even if we don't have spouses and children to deal with. They considered our voices important when talking about families, a discussion we were usually left out of. I was trying to hide the tears that were streaming down my face in this seemingly nonemotional meeting. I would love to see the church rise up to bring more valida- tion to the singles in their own congregations in similar ways.

Though there have been occasions like the past two examples that have made me feel validated as a single person, ninety percent of the time I have felt overlooked in my disenfranchised grief in the church. I don't feel like I get a lot of good support or information that helps me cope with being thirty-something and single.

It helps me to remember that even when no one around me understands my pain, God understands. He doesn't want me to dwell in it or drown in it, but he does wants to meet me were I am and let me know that he understands.

One of the stories that has ministered the most to me in this season of being single is the story of Hannah, the mother of Samuel. Hannah's name means "Beautiful" or "Passionate," both very befitting. She was one of two wives of a man named Elkanah. Elkanah's other wife was named Peninnah. Peninnah had many children, but Hannah was barren.

Every year, the family would go to offer a sacrifice at the temple called Shiloh. Elkanah would give Hannah a double portion because he loved her, and he mourned with her that she couldn't have children.

Peninnah was cruel to Hannah, however, and would mock her for not having any children. You can imagine what she might have said to Hannah: "Where is your God now? He seems to have blessed me and kept you barren. I wonder why that's happening to you. Maybe you did something wrong? Maybe you're not good enough?" Does that sound familiar?

Hannah would weep bitterly and mourn so much that she wouldn't be able to eat anything.

Her husband would come to her and say, "Hannah, why are you weeping? Why don't you eat? Why are you downhearted? Don't I mean more to you than ten sons?" Though she knew that her husband loved her, she still mourned over what she did not have. She longed for a child.

She went to the temple and made a vow to the Lord. She said, "O Lord Almighty, if you will only look upon your servant's misery, and remember me, and not forget your servant but give her a son, then I will give him to the Lord for all the days of his life."

The priest, Eli, saw Hannah in all of her passion. He was not used to seeing someone worship by crying out in this way, so he assumed she was drunk.

He admonished her, but she said, "I am a woman who is deeply troubled. I have not been drinking. I was pouring out my soul to the Lord. Do not take your servant for a wicked woman; I have been praying here out of my great anguish and grief."

Eli said, "Go in peace, and may the God of Israel grant you what you have asked of him" (1 Samuel 1:11, 17, NIV).

Then she went and ate something, and her face was

no longer downcast. Notice here that even before her prayer was answered, she lifted her head. The simple act of pouring out her heart to God gave her hope.

The next day, she woke up and worshipped with her husband. And then they went home.

In the course of time, God joyfully answered Hannah's prayer. She conceived and bore a son and named him Samuel. Samuel means "God heard me."

When her son was born, she worshipped God with this beautiful prayer:

> My heart rejoices in the Lord; in the Lord is my horn lifted high. My mouth boasts over my enemies, for I delight in your deliverance. There is no one holy like the Lord; there is no one besides you; there is no Rock like our God [. . .] *the Lord is a God who knows* [. . .] He raises the poor from the dust and lifts the needy from the ash heap; he seats them with princes and has them inherit a throne of honor. (1 Samuel 2:1-3,8, NIV, emphasis mine.)

In some ways, her prayer was more than worship. It was prophesy. When Hannah prayed this prayer, kings did not exist in her nation; judges were the leaders of Israel in that era. She was, perhaps, foreseeing that this son that God gave her would do great things, including anointing the first two kings of Israel, Saul and David, bringing them into their reign.

In the next few years, Hannah conceived three more sons and two daughters, but she kept her promise to God with her first son. Samuel grew up in the temple. Samuel was born as a result of his mother's worship, so it made sense that he would be raised in a place of worship.

Samuel was raised by Eli, the priest. Eli had many sons who were also priests, but they were evil. Samuel, however, heard and followed God's voice from a very young age. In a long line of corrupt leaders, he grew up to be a political leader who ruled by listening to God.

Samuel was the bridge of the old era to a new era because he was considered the last judge of Israel and the first prophet of Israel. The political atmosphere of Israel completely changed with Samuel. It went from a place where judgement ruled to a place where listening and responding to God ruled. Just as God did not judge Hannah but listened to her, Samuel was able to access a God who not only judged, but who also listened.

A nation was changed forever, and it all came from a hurting woman who didn't hide her disappointment from God but who poured it out to him instead.[15]

Do you know what I love most about this story? I love that Hannah let herself mourn. I love that when she described what she was going through, she used words like "great anguish and grief," "misery," and "deeply troubled." Have you felt pain that deep before? I know that I have. Have you been like me, trying to cover up how raw and real those emotions are? Avoiding words that really describe how much you ache? Hiding your pain from God because you fear that you would seem ungrateful if you questioned why your life doesn't make sense to you at times?

About eight years ago, I bought a dining room table from a thrift store for my birthday. The table was very dusty, but when I rubbed off some of the dust, I saw how beautiful it was. It was made of dark wood, with claw and ball legs and chairs with flowers etched into them. I don't often spend money on myself; I felt foolish even wanting the table. But in my mind's eye, as clear as day as I stood in that thrift store, I saw myself sitting with a family around that table. I saw us talking about our days. I saw friends who had come over having deep conversations with us over dinner. I saw children running around, playing hide-and-go-seek, laughing.

I bought that table as a gift of hope to myself. I had great expectation that those things would happen around that very table.

My brother and sister-in-law had the table for a few years since I was traveling throughout California and was not in a stable home for a season. After a while, they decided to move away, and I couldn't afford to come get the table. They wanted to sell it. I kicked and scratched. I did not want to sell that table. I thought maybe my older brother would take it, but he didn't. There wasn't room for the table in my new house. I knew that I had to let it go.

The table was worth some money, but it wasn't in the best shape. I put ads up, asking for eight hundred dollars. I talked about how priceless the table was, how beautiful. No one budged. Down to five hundred. And down and down and down.

My sister-in-law called me and said, "Kate, you've got to stop talking about how amazing that table is. You will get more money for it if you say that it is crap."

Finally, my brother sold it at a garage sale for two hundred dollars.

It was more than a table to me. It was attached to my dreams. Nearly a decade after buying the table, those dreams had not come to pass. They were sold at a garage sale for a couple hundred bucks.

I believe that when that table was sold, God did for me what he did for Hannah. He did not mock my sadness over a piece of furniture. He knew it was not a little thing to me. He knew that I was disappointed, and he let me mourn.

God did not say to Hannah, "You are so ungrateful! You have a husband who loves you. Isn't that enough?" as her husband points out. Nor did he say, "Be still, my child. Know that I am God. I, and only I, am to fill this empty place in you."

No, God did not answer her that way. He heard her prayer. He heard the cry of her heart and he understood. He listened. And I believe he ached with her, just as he has ached with me the hundred times I have cried out to him. He understood that no matter how much she loved her God, there was still a deep aching in her because she didn't have a physical, flesh-and-blood child.

As she poured out her anguish to the Lord, she worshipped. After she poured out her sorrow, she worshipped in a different way. Even before he gave her a child, she worshipped. And then, he answered her. He gave her a son. He is the God who hears. And just like in Hannah's prayer, "He is the God who knows."

Like it was with Hannah, it is valid for me to say, "I don't believe this is my fault. It is something I don't understand. And it aches so much, Lord. Please, please, hear my cry. But in the midst of this trial, I still choose to worship you."

Thankfulness and grieving don't have to be mutually exclusive. We can be thankful while simultaneously allowing ourselves to mourn when we need to. We need a balance between these two things.

When God talks to me, he calls me Katie Girl. Writing that name makes me teary, because it brings to mind a lifetime of journeys I have walked with the Lord. I know my Father's heart when I hear that name. I remember how much he loves me when I hear that name.

The other day, I was journaling out what I was hearing from God, like a letter from him. It is something I often do when I need to hear his tender voice. I had just experienced a difficult rejection from someone whom I cared deeply about, and I was weeping much like Hannah wept. I asked him the question I have asked more than any other in my life: "Lord, why do my relationships end in a broken heart instead of in a covenant? Why has no one fallen in love with me in such a long time? It aches so much. It doesn't seem right."

This is what he said: "Katie Girl, you have been faithful to believe in my goodness even after a very long time of praying for a family. You are so strong and so patient. I am not letting go of you, love. You will not be left unrewarded for your faithfulness to me. I keep all of my promises."

He did not say, "Now, Kate, you aren't trusting me in this place." He did not say, "Look at all that you *do* have, Kate. Be grateful for heaven's sake!" Yes, I do need to trust. Yes, I do need to be thankful. Yes, I do need to let go of that table for a season. Maybe I will need to let go of it for my whole life. But in that moment, God knew that I needed to mourn.

He did not tell me that I was weak. He told me that I was strong. So strong that I refused to let go of him, just like Hannah did. That is what I needed to hear in that moment.

As my song "Love of My Life" says,

> You are strong even in your weakness
> Even then you're lovely
> You are strong because I see you holy
> When you're covered in my love
>
> I weep when you're reaching from me
> I weep 'cause you love me blind
> You're the one—the one I'd die for
> You're the love, the love of my life[16]

God does not see me weak. Even when I am weeping bitterly, he sees me strong. He sees me beautiful. He does not mock my pain. He bends down to hold me when I cry. I would venture to say that he cries with me not only because he aches with me, but also because he is so proud of the way I have trusted him through this, one of the longest, hardest trials of my life. Because, like the song says, I have loved him blind.

He also loves me blind. He loves me even in my weakness. He sees past my questioning and my frustration and my ranting, and he sees me faithful.

If you are experiencing this kind of grief, I think God is looking upon you with mercy right now. He is giving you permission to grieve. He is giving you permission to have compassion on yourself and to know that you are experiencing a true, deep loss. Even if it is a "disenfranchised loss," it is a grief that is real and painful.

He sees you trying to trust him, and it means so much.

Tomorrow, after we have allowed ourselves time to mourn, it would be wise for us to wake up, take a shower, have coffee with some friends, eat a salad instead of a pint of Ben and Jerry's, and remember that life is still beautiful. If we don't choose to have a balance, we will get really depressed.

We don't want to be stuck in this grief on a constant basis. We don't want to rant forever.

But now, just for a little while, we can crawl into our Daddy's lap, let him call us by name, and remember that *he is the God who knows.*

We need to let him sing this song to us:

> *Lay your weary head down now*
> *Let me hold you, hold you like a little child*
> *You don't have to be strong*
> *I will be strong for you*
> *You don't have to say a word, love*
> *Being close to you is all I want*
> *Rest here in my love*
> *'Til it's enough for you*
>
> *Be still and know*
> *Quiet your soul*
> *In this world you will have trouble*
> *But take heart—I have overcome*
> *I have overcome*
>
> *Let me hold you close and hold you still*
> *Know I love you and I always will*

You don't have to hold on
I will hold on to you
Be still and know
Quiet your soul[17]

Chapter Four

The Lonely Doll

I remember very clearly the first book I ever read. I was four years old and sitting on our yellow shag carpet next to a big picture window. It was early evening. My mom had checked out the book from the library earlier in the week, and I had already looked through it several times. Mom sat next to me and pointed to the words, sounding them out one by one. Something clicked in my mind; I suddenly understood what it meant to read. I had already learned the alphabet, but now I grasped that when I put letters together, they made words.

At the time, I didn't realize that what I had just learned would change my life. All I knew was that when I started sounding out the words by myself, my mom was so proud of me. In fact, on that first night before I went to bed, she gave me a rice candy as a reward for learning to read. Reading the words of that book and receiving that reward is my most vivid memory from that age.

The main character of the book was a little doll named Edith. I vaguely remember that the doll lived in a big house and was very lonely. More than anything in the world, she wanted friends. I remember her being blonde and pretty, with little hoop earrings, and I remember that she had the same look on her face in every picture.

You see, Edith was a real doll, and the pictures of her weren't drawn but photographed. She was placed in poses around the author's house and all over New York, and the author used the pictures to weave stories together. The photographs made Edith seem so real, as if the stories were not mere make-believe. As if the doll could have been my next door neighbor. As if I could have knocked on her door and said, "I'm lonely sometimes, too. Let's be friends."

What I realize now is that I didn't just learn how to read that day, I learned what to *expect*. Words make stories. Stories shape beliefs. Beliefs shape lives. The words of that little storybook had me believing at a very young age that I would have a happy ending in which I wasn't lonely anymore, just like the lonely doll.

A few weeks ago, I was thinking about the book and how much it influenced me. I wondered if I could hunt it down on the internet, but I could not remember the name of the author or even the title of the book. A few days later, one my favorite radio programs, *This American Life*, aired a story about Dare Wright, a children's book author who was at the height of her fame in the late 1950s. The story discussed Miss Wright's life and how it paralleled the stories that she wrote. Within a few minutes, I realized that the book they were talking about—her most famous book—was *my* book, the first book I had ever read. It was called *The Lonely Doll*. I was fascinated, and I went home to do more research.[18]

I discovered that Dare was a beautiful but troubled woman. She got engaged after a five year courtship, but her fiancé called off the wedding, and soon after doing so he died in a plane crash. Dare was so devastated that she spoke out loud to pictures of him the rest of her life.

Soon after his death, Dare took pictures of her childhood doll and wrote these little stories. She changed the doll to look more like herself: straight blonde hair in a low ponytail and hoop earrings like she always wore and clothes that were similar to her own. Dare's method of easing her mourning was brilliant: she created a character that looked just like herself—a character who was as lonely as she was—and then she gave that character a happy ending.[19]

Let's look at the stories that Dare wrote. Little Edith, the doll, "lived in a nice house and had everything she needed except somebody to play with." She lived in New York, just like the author. Edith begged two pigeons on the windowsill to be her friends, but they flew away.

Edith knelt at her bed and we read, "Every night when she said her prayers, she pleaded, 'Please, please send me some friends.'" Soon the little doll's prayers were answered as two real-life stuffed F.A.O. Schwartz teddy bears move in with her: a papa bear and a brother bear. And with these two new companions, Edith was not alone anymore.[20]

I related to the little doll just like the author did. I, too, was aching with loneliness.

My elementary school days were especially lonely.

During that time, my parents went through a very difficult divorce. So difficult, in fact, that twenty-five years later they still don't like being in the same room. My little heart was shattered at their divorce. My parents have been attentive at different points of my life, but during the divorce they themselves were struggling with so much pain that they didn't seem to know how to deal with mine.

My school life was almost as difficult as my home life was. I was a shy little girl. Recess was the worst time of the day for me because it reminded me that I was alone. I would wander around the playground aimlessly, trying to pass the time. I remember standing on the hill overlooking my classmates, all of whom didn't look very lonely, moving my thrift store coat zipper up and down and praying. It was a prayer very similar to Edith's prayer: "Please, please send me some friends. I don't want to be lonely anymore."

Now that I am an adult, my childhood prayer has been answered a hundredfold. I have had incredible friends in my life. I have had spiritual parents who have nurtured me and who have talked on the phone with me when I was going through breakups or depressions. I have had countless strangers who have taken me in while I was on music tours, who have fed me, and who have taken time out of their schedules to get to know me. I have had friends who have brought me meals and knee-high socks to comfort me, friends who went shopping for me and cried with me when I was sick.

But I have a new thing I ask God for that hasn't been answered yet.

I stand on the hill overlooking my life. I move the zipper on my fashionable black winter jacket up and down. I look at the people below me with their careers and their spouses and their Facebook pictures of their beautiful children.

"Please, please send me a family," I pray. "I don't want to be lonely anymore."

I forget that I have friends and family all around me because I am so focused on the far away people and their seemingly perfect lives. I compare my insides with their outsides, a comparison that is never helpful or accurate.

People always smile in pictures, but that doesn't mean that they are actually that happy in real life. If I were to stop feeling so sorry for myself and climb down that hill, I would realize that their lives aren't perfect, either. I would probably discover that many of these people are often lonely like me. We might even be able to comfort each other in our loneliness.

Stories that have a similar plot line to *The Lonely Doll* are told to us over and over again, first as children and then as adults. In the same radio story that talked about Dare Wright, there was an interview with long-time Kindergarten teacher and author Vivian Paley. Dr. Paley has extensively studied the stories children make up. In it, she says that when young children are asked to tell a story, they usually say something like, "There was a little rabbit that lived in the woods and he was very lonely. Then a fox came and became friends with the rabbit and they weren't lonely anymore." And then the next child will say something like, "There was a car that was very very lonely. Then a truck came along and became the car's friend. They played together and then they weren't lonely."

According to Paley, the children tell different versions of this same story again and again. And interestingly, the listening children don't say, "Enough already! Why do you keep telling the same story?" Instead, they say, "More, more!"[21]

Clearly, even at a young age there is something innate in human beings that doesn't like being alone. Even as children we understand that we were made for relationship. God designed it that way. We were born into families in which someone else has to care for us in order for us to survive. But somehow along the way, even as young as these children telling their stories, we realize that our relationships are fragile and can be easily broken. We understand that human beings can suffer rejection and loneliness.

These school children sensed that loneliness and disconnect are not good, so they told their stories about their little lonely characters meeting someone that loves them, just like Dare Wright told the story of the lonely doll.

Even as adults we hear this same story again and again. There is a good reason that we are told the story so many times: it makes a lot of money. In Steven Pressfield's book *The War of Art*, he talks about the motto of a big advertising agency: "Invent a disease. Come up with the disease, and we can sell the cure."[22] I don't think it would be a stretch to say that Hollywood has greatly benefited from a disease called loneliness. They have sold a cure, and it is called romance.

Here is a sampling of the stories that have been told to us as adults:

> *Once upon a time in the 1980s, there were two lonely people named Harry and Sally. They hated each other at first, but later they became best friends. Then they had a big fight. Then they fell in love and they weren't lonely anymore.*

Next story:

> *Once upon a time in the 1990s, a sleepless man in Seattle talked about being a lonely widower on a radio show. A cute, lonely blonde girl decided she was madly in love with him, even though she had never met him. Then they met on top of the Empire State Building and they weren't lonely anymore.*

And the next story:

> *Once upon a time in the 2000s, two lonely people who looked remarkably like the characters in the last story anonymously emailed each other very clever love letters. Neither one of them realized that they were enemies in real life. They figured out that they loved each other, and then they weren't lonely anymore. They seemed to have forgotten that they already met each other ten years ago on top of the Empire State Building.*[23]

Do you see how similar these movie plots are to the

children's stories that Dare Wright wrote and Dr. Paley observed? The lonely doll has been replaced by lonely adult men and women who find each other and have happy endings. We are told this story over and over again, and we never seem to get tired of it. We clap our hands and say, "More, more!"

It would be wise for us to recognize our disease of loneliness and realize that getting married will not cure that disease. Real life is nothing like storybooks or chick flicks. There are no producers to come up with a predictable plot. No editors to cut out the parts you don't like. There are no writers that will answer every question and bring resolution to every challenge.

Your life won't have a perfectly hemmed-in ending. It will be ripped and tattered and re-sewn like a patchwork quilt. Marriage, singleness, divorce, loneliness, joy—these are the pieces of fabric that might make up that quilt. Whether God is the one who created the hard patches is not a question that I can answer. But I do believe this: God is the thread. Your life is stitched with the color of his mercy, his grace, his love.

You may never understand why you are lonely on this earth. But one day, God will hold out that quilt for you, and he will say, "Look what I made for you. Isn't it beautiful?" Then he will wrap the quilt around you, hold you close, and say, "There you go, love. You don't have to be lonely anymore."

That, my friends, will be the ending to your story. It is the happiest one you could ever imagine.

Chapter Five

The Trouble With Expectations

I am writing this chapter as I sit at a park bench in front of the library in my charming Colorado town. I've been here for about an hour and a half. It is a Friday night in September. I rode my bike here, and it is perfect outside: the sun is setting and there is a street fair two blocks away, complete with outdoor rollerskating.

The library closed at 6 p.m., like it does every Friday. I came hoping to do some research, but I got here too late and now I am a little disappointed that it is closed. My expectations weren't met. I expected to be inside reading something riveting, but because it was closed, I am now sitting on a bench near the front doors of the library. My disappointment is quickly dissipating, however, because it is so lovely outside.

As I sit here writing, though, something intriguing is happening before my eyes. One by one people approach the automatic doors and wait for them to open. They realize the library is locked, they look at the sign on the window— the closed sign, mind you— and they walk away, clearly disappointed. A little girl starts crying because she wants to have story time with her mom. A teenager cusses under his breath. A little boy who has to use the bathroom starts whining. I have counted nine people who expected to go to the library but couldn't get in. None of them could do anything about the locked doors, and none of them liked it. I wonder if this happens every Friday night.

As if on cue, a tall man with long white hair and a yellow T-shirt comes to the door of the library with books in hand. The automatic doors don't open, and he says out loud, "What?!" Then he starts yelling over and over again, "What?! What?!" He is mad. I mean really mad. It is kind of hilarious.

I feel like a spy right now because I am typing about him as he walks back and forth in a rage right in front of me. He has no idea that his ridiculous reaction to a library being closed is being immortalized in literature as he paces.

Dude, it's a library. There's a book drop twenty feet away. It will be open again at 9 a.m. Put your books in the book drop, go down the street, and enjoy the street fair.

It seems pointless to get angry at a little thing like the library being closed. But this is what happens when you are consumed by unmet expectations. If you're not careful, your expectations will steal away your joy.

In many ways, I look as ridiculous as this man. I come to the library where all the stories of my expectations are written. The story I dreamed of as a little girl, of friends coming and rescuing me from my loneliness. The story I wanted as a teenager, of a close-knit family rescuing me from my loneliness. The story I pray for as an adult, of a man who deeply loves me, rescuing me from my loneliness.

I stand at the doors of these expectations and they are locked.

"What?! What?!" I yell. "I want in! Why are these doors closed? This is not what I expected! This is not what I thought life would look like! I am outside the doors, and I am lonely. What do I do with this loneliness? With this emptiness?"

The hard truth is that even if I walk through those locked doors and over the threshold of marriage, I will struggle with disappointment. In fact, the greater my expectations about marriage, the more disappointed I will be.

My friend Tim said to me the other day, "Kate, if there is one thing I can guarantee about being married and having children, it's that it won't be anything like you expected."

I want to clap my hands over my ears and say, "No, no! Don't tell me that!"

But I would be wise to take my hands off my ears and listen to what he says, to realize that it is practically guaranteed that our lives will most likely look much different than we expect they will. I mean, when has life ever come about in the way you expected it to?

As I said in the last chapter, we often create stories about what romance and marriage will look like. Stories are not necessarily bad things; they have been a central part of every culture since the beginning of time. But we live in a society where the stories we create do not give us a realistic view of what life in covenant looks like. We have to be careful about what we do with the expectations our made-up stories create.

If you are like me and have watched 1246 chick flicks, you have started to think that the boy-meets-girl formula is the answer you've been looking for since you were a child. You have believed that the loneliness will be gone when you fall in love and get married, just like it was for Harry and Sally, with their wedding cake that has chocolate sauce on the side. With every story you hear, you have built up more expectation for what your own love story will look like.

In fact, I expect that the degree of resentment you may one day have in a marriage will be directly proportional to the unrealistic expectations that you have now.

In an article called "The Expectation Trap" in *Psychology Today*, author Hara Estroff Marano discusses how our culture has inundated us with the idea that all of our happiness can be found in our spouse. Marriage in other centuries was more centered around a woman being provided for and around raising a family than it was around love and intimacy. Throughout history, there was more of a sense of duty attached to marriage rather than there was romance. Marano says, "It wasn't until the 18th century that anyone thought that love might have anything to do with marriage."

She continues,

> Because our intimate relationships are now almost wholly vehicles for meeting our

emotional needs, and with almost all our
emotions invested in one [person], we tend to
look upon any unhappiness we experience whatever the source—as a failure of a partner to
satisfy your longings.

Disappointment inevitably feels so *personal*. We
see no other possibility but to hunt for indi-
vidual psychological reason-that is, to blame our
partners for our own unhappiness. But much
of the discontent we now encounter in close
relationship is culturally inflicted, although we
rarely interpret our experience that way. An
accumulation of forces has made the cultural
climate hostile to long term relationships today.

She goes on to say that our culture has created an atmosphere where we feel the need to constantly monitor our
own happiness. When we are not happy, we blame our
lack of happiness on our spouse or on other people around
us. We don't often look to ourselves or to what we have
contributed to the dysfunction.

In the same article, William Doherty, professor of
family sciences at the University of Minnesota agrees:
"People work themselves up over the ordinary problems
of marriage, for which, by the way, they usually fail to
see their own contributions. They badger their partners to
change, convince themselves nothing will budge, and so
work their way out of really good relationships."[24]

This is the trouble with expectations. If we are not
careful, we will set ourselves up for disappointment and

we may possibly sabotage good relationships. We would do well to listen to the advice that this doctor gives even before we are married. To work hard not to let our hopes be completely wrapped up in the person we may marry some day. To put boundaries on our expectations and not see marriage as a vehicle through which all of our needs will be met. That was never what marriage was meant to be.

I have had several married friends tell me lately that there is a deep loneliness that happens when you finally get married. It is a different kind of loneliness than what you experience as a single person. When you are single, the sentiment is, "when I get married, this aching in me will be filled." When you are married, it often becomes, "I am married now, and this aching in me is still not filled. If this doesn't fill it, what will?" I have been told that this happens in even the happiest of marriages. It is something that we should prepare ourselves for.

Let's look at what Jesus says about expectations in Matthew 6:25-34:

> Therefore I tell you, do not worry about your
> life, what you will eat or drink; or about your
> body, what you will wear [. . .] Look at the
> birds of the air; they do not sow or reap or
> store away in barns, and yet your heavenly
> Father feeds them. Are you not much more
> valuable than they? Who of you by worrying
> can add a single hour to his life? And why
> do you worry about clothes? See how the lilies
> of the field grow. They do not labor or spin.

Yet I tell you that not even Solomon in all his splendor was dressed like one of these. If that is how God clothes the grass of the field, which is here today and tomorrow is thrown into the fire, will he not much more clothe you, O you of little faith! So do not worry, saying, 'What shall we eat?' or 'What shall we drink?' or 'What shall we wear?' For the pagans run after all these things, and your heavenly Father knows that you need them. But seek first his kingdom and his righteousness, and all these things will be given to you as well. Therefore do not worry about tomorrow, for tomorrow will worry about itself. Each day has enough trouble of its own. (NIV)

Notice that Jesus doesn't say, "It would be a good idea not to worry about tomorrow." He says, "*Do not* worry about tomorrow." He commands it. It appears that Jesus is not really into projecting futures. It seems that instead, he thinks it is really wise to be present today, grateful for the people in your life at this moment, holding them closely and with love but holding them with open hands. It is wise to trust God with your future without expecting your future to look a certain way.

I am learning to take my life one day at a time, rather than to project all of my hope onto a distant future. When that distant future comes, even if it involves a happy marriage, I probably won't feel that much more satisfied than I do today.

As Henri Nouwen states in his book, *The Wounded Healer,*

We easily relate to our human world with devastating expectations. We ignore what we already know [. . .] that no love or friend-ship, no intimate embrace or tender kiss, no community, commune or collective, no man or woman, will ever be able to satisfy our desire to be released from our lonely condition.[25]

So if we aren't able to place our expectations for happiness in marriage, what should we put our hope in?

I know that the pat answer is to hope in God. Indeed, I have loved God for a very long time. I cannot deny for a second that he has given me hope and meaning. When I think about where my life would be without him, I am amazed at how much joy he has given me—I am amazed at how knowing him has saved me from a life of abuse and despair. I will never fully know how my relationship with him has affected my life until I am in heaven.

But sometimes, even though the constancy of this hope is there, I still feel a deep aching. Life doesn't always feel right to me. When someone I love is sick, when I am around my street friends who have lived such hard lives, when I am having a hard day and just want someone to hold me, when a friend goes through a divorce, when I can barely look at a child without wanting to cry, life doesn't feel right. Because it's not right. We are longing for heaven. The hard truth is, God never promised that we wouldn't have seasons of aching in this life.

But he did promise us this: "'Though the mountains be shaken and the hills be removed, yet my unfailing love for you will not be shaken nor my covenant of peace be removed,' says the Lord, who has compassion on you" (Isaiah 54:10, NIV).

This is not some vague thought. It is a promise. No matter what happens, his love for us will not be shaken. That is something that is perfectly reasonable to hope in, because it is guaranteed.

I might be single for a long time—maybe for the rest of my life. I might love people who end up leaving me. I might get sick. People I care about could die. But no one, nothing, can take away the love that God has for me. Ever. That may not be a truth that will completely take away my feelings of loneliness. But it is, nevertheless, a truth that gives me a reason to live.

Life will not always meet my expectations. But there is one thing that I can always expect: that I will be loved by my Creator. I can never lose his love. That promise is something I can always put my hope in.

Maybe I should stop focusing on the locked doors and go down the street to the fair instead. To the place that is not locked to me. To the place that is near to me at this very moment. It's possible that I will get to go into the library tomorrow, but today, I should stand in wonder at the beautiful sunset outside of those locked doors.

I want to move beyond expectations to a place of acceptance. Beyond unrealistic stories to a place of deeper, richer realities. Beyond loneliness to a place of rest and joyful solitude.

I would be wise to stop looking for my happy ending and start living in my happy today.

HOW TO HAVE A PROMISING FUTURE
↪Special Education

1.) Try to look at the fruit of something when it is still a seed.

2.) Do the next right thing.

Chapter Six

Confession, Reality TV, and the Space in Between

I have a secret to tell you. It is a secret I have only told a few of my closest friends. It is such a stunning secret that I never even hinted at it to my last boyfriend, and I told him pretty much everything about my life. But not this. I knew that his view of me would change if I told him.

Before I confess this secret to you, let me explain that minor panic sets in whenever I hear the word *confession*. This goes back many years, to my Catholic upbringing.

I really didn't like going to mass when I was a kid, which is the Catholic word for the weekly service. My love for God didn't accompany the tradition at the time, and so the services didn't often come alive for me. I didn't like saying the same words over and over again. I didn't like the kneeling and getting up and kneeling and getting up, like a room full of un-smiling jack-in-the-boxes.

My brother and I would try desperately to make the long hour of mass pass more quickly. We would hold our breath, timing each other to see who could hold it the longest. We would draw little faces on our fingers and put on puppet shows, trying not to laugh. We even had a special secret handshake for the part of the service when everyone shakes hands and says, "Peace be with you."

My brother set a bulletin on fire once. Definitely made that particular mass less boring.

The thing I dreaded the most about being Catholic was not the mass, however. It was confession. You know, like in the movies where you go behind a screen and tell the priest all of your deepest darkest sins. Except we didn't have a screen. We had to look Father Murphy straight in the face.

It was terrifying.

I had a secret back then, too; one that I was very scared of confessing. I was a kleptomaniac. I would go in a store with used grocery bags in my coat, fill a basket with makeup and chocolates, go into the bathroom, put the loot in the bags, and walk out of the store. It was brilliant, really. I stole so many chocolates that to this day, I can tell you the filling of any Russell Stover chocolate just by their shape. My brothers and I would would also use this method to steal key lime pies and eat them in the parking lot.

I remember standing in the line for confession, wondering what to do. Should I tell the priest that I stole everything I could get my hands on, including things like a $1500 pearl necklace from the people I babysat for? How would I tell him? Would eight Hail Marys really absolve what I had done? Should I just skip confessing this particular sin and pretend that I was a better person than I really was?

I remember the conversation going like this: "Forgive me, Father, for I have sinned." Cue lots of crying on my part. "I steal things. Mostly sugary things. My mom doesn't let us have sugary things, and I just can't help myself. I love truffles! I love key lime pie! I would give up the key lime pie, Father, but not the chocolates. Please, please, don't make me give up the chocolates!"

Side note: As an adult, I still have a minor obsession with chocolate, but now my tastes have been refined to really good dark chocolate. I buy it with my hard-earned money instead of sticking it in my coat, though, just in case you were wondering.

My Catholic upbringing was the first leg of my faith journey. I have had many adventures along the way since then, and each part of the path has brought me through a variety of different denominations. Over the years, I have been a member of conservative community churches, Evangelical-Free-turned-ultra-charismatic churches, house churches, and edgy, artsy social justice churches. I honestly don't know much about the doctrines of any of these denominations; I just know that I love Jesus and that I look for family wherever I am.

However, in the last few years, I have found a new depth and resonance for my faith in the same place that I started this journey: in ancient traditions and mystical ponderings that mimic that of the Catholic faith. I have a newfound love for these ancient traditions, and they have been a rich part of my recent spiritual life.

I credit this new love to an internship I did with Inner-CHANGE. InnerCHANGE is my favorite organization I have worked with, and I am praying about working with them full-time. I worked with one team in San Francisco whose goal was to minister to young homeless people in Golden Gate Park. I befriended street kids and ate meals with them in our home. I taught a music class with young homeless people and made an album of their music. Our team chose to be homeless for three days in order to understand better what life on the streets is like. It was one of the most eye-opening experiences of my life.

In InnerCHANGE, each missionary patterns the rhythm of his or her life in traditionally monastic ways, making sure there is rest and fellowship built into the week so no one gets burnt out with the ministry work. Each missionary goes on solitude retreats every six months to either a monastery or to a hermitage. (Yes, there are still hermits. In fact, the hermit I met at Sky Farm Hermitage in California was one of the warmest people I've ever met. Her life consists of hosting guests, gardening, praying for peace, and saying wonderful, wise things in a voice like that of a Disney character. She's beautiful.)

Since interning with InnerCHANGE, I have made visiting monasteries and hermitages a part of my lifestyle. I've visited five monasteries from Ireland to Colorado to Big Sur, California, in the last two years. These monasteries are beautiful, serene places where I can set apart time to listen to God. To hear his heartbeat. I love it.

I have also fallen in love with the writings of Henri

Nouwen, who was Catholic as well. I can't get enough of him. I feel like he's my soul mate. Forget that he was a priest and that he's not alive anymore; he is still my soul mate, at least in my literary world. I have been reading other books by Catholic monks and priests and nuns. These authors are no longer a joke to me. They are people who have dedicated their lives to loving God, and they have a lot of wisdom to give. They have unique, beautiful ways of looking at the world that help me to see things differently.

After many years of going to churches that were worried about having one smidgen of silence in their services, I have been refreshed by the quietness of contemplation. I have loved feeling like I can come to God and be silent with him. I have loved just letting him love me. My faith journey has seemed to come full circle when it comes to denominations. Back to the deep faith of an ancient church.

It felt really good to write the last few paragraphs. You know why? Because I just described a part of me that I especially like. The part that deeply loves Jesus and deeply loves people that are hurting, not to mention the part that is cool enough to be homeless for a few days. In my mind, you now know the "good" part of me. The part that I think will impress you.

I would like to make you believe that the deep, beautiful, mystical Kate is who I am all the time. To convince you that there is no such thing as the weak, insecure Kate.

But your view of me is about to change, because the dreaded confession that I mentioned at the beginning of this chapter is coming. Right now, my bedroom is like the confession room and my Macbook Pro is my virtual Catholic priest and our conversation might go something like

this: "Forgive me, Father MacBook Pro, for I have sinned."
I pour out my heart to the screen and it responds, "Your
sin has been absolved, my daughter. Buy three iphone apps
and live in peace."

Making this confession is especially scary to me, because
you are now going to know a part of me that I don't like
very much.

OK. Here I go. Here is my secret:

I watch *The Bachelor.*

"Are you kidding?" you say. "All this talk of childhood
kleptomania and a Catholic confession digression and
Russell Stover . . . you're going to write all of that to lead
up to your deepest darkest secret and it's watching a TV
show? I thought we would get something really gossip-
worthy, like that you were secretly dating a Brazilian
diplomat or that you're a double agent or something."

But you see, watching *The Bachelor* makes me feel like
I am much shallower than I make myself out to be. I
honestly would rather have admitted that I used to be a
drug dealer. You just read about how I worked with this
incredible organization helping street kids. You read about
how I have become much more of a centered person. You
read about how I spend time meditating and having solitude retreats and meeting hermits and monks and reading
Henri Nouwen. But now that you know the truth, you
won't remember any of the good stuff; you will only
remember me as that author girl who shallowly watches
The Bachelor.

A person who watches *The Bachelor?* Not mystical. They
are one step up from soap opera addicts.

I think I have felt especially secretive about watching

this show because for most of my adult life, I haven't been a big TV watcher. I grew up watching too much TV, so when I got older, I kind of hated it. I looked at people who always had the TV on and thought of them as lazy. I was better than them. I read books instead of watching TV. I wasn't going to give into popular culture—not now, not ever. I would not be materialistic. I would not listen to Top 40 pop songs that aren't hip enough for me. I would be counter-culture. I would be deep. I would be a super-non-TV-watching-got-over-my-kleptomania-intriguing-indie-music-listening-mystical-social-justice-loving-follower-of-Jesus-who-wears-Toms-shoes.

But during the last few years, when I was in ministry school and being taught about spiritual things all the time, when I was working with homeless people and feeling so sad for them, when I was touring and meeting so many people that I was sapped of all my energy, well, sometimes I just wanted to stop thinking.

During these difficult seasons, I realized that I could have TV on my own laptop and hide it a little more. It became less of a social event and more of a private event. So I started watching it. And *The Bachelor* became my one staple TV show.

I know, I know. If I'm going to watch one show, why would I choose this one? It is just ridiculous. Every season it is the same. The man with the perfect chest and perfect charm. The synthetically-endowed, bikini-wearing, bleached-hair-perfect, gorgeous women. Some of them are sweet; some of them are psycho. In fact, I heard a radio program in which a reality show producer admitted to trying to cast forty percent narcissists and people who are crazy enough to make good television but not crazy enough to bash the camera in with a bat. I wish I could find the reference for you so you could hear it too, but I can't.

Every season the same scenes repeat over and over throughout the episode ("Next, on *The Bachelor* . . ."), so that they can fill two hours and get a lot of money from advertisers. There are the same make-out sessions with a boatload of girls. And there is always the same saga of the man being totally torn by his deep love for two (or three or four) women, all of whom he's known for about five weeks. And host Chris Harrison always, always says, "And now, for the most shocking ending in *The Bachelor* history." I mean, it's ridiculous.

And for some mysterious reason, I love every minute of it.

I admit, I have a problem. I all but tap my arm before I shoot myself up with a new season. Why, I ask myself? Why would I want to watch this show?

In order to feel less shallow, I like to tell myself that I'm not just watching TV; I am observing a sociological experiment. I ask myself with a very scientific air, "What is the psychological process of a man who is put into a room with a number of beautiful women? When he has to choose who he wants to break up with and who he wants to keep?" I convince myself that I'm a lot like Jane Goodall, only instead of watching monkeys and the way they interact, I'm observing a bunch of hot people.

I'm not watching this for entertainment, people! I'm watching it for research! Under my blanket and with my headphones on, so my housemates won't hear the mumbling of romantic TV encounters coming from under the door. What's wrong with that?

I am learning that other people share this same secret. Recently, I mentioned a character on *The Bachelor* to one of my best friends and covered my mouth when I realized my mistake.

"You watch *The Bachelor*?" she asked.

Sheepishly, I replied, "Yes, yes I do," as if I were admitting to being a kleptomaniac or something.

"I do, too!" she said.

"What?"

"I've always watched it in secret because I was afraid of what people would think of me if they knew."

"Me too!"

"Are you kidding? We could have been watching it together this whole time!"

I've met more and more people with the same secret addiction, even married couples who are pastors. Maybe we can all get together and create a support group or something where I could ease my conscience by saying "Hi, I'm Kate, and I am a Bacheloraholic."

So there. I've said it. I've told you my secret. It's out in the open. I feel absolved. Thank you, Father Macbook Pro. Thank you.

I feel surprisingly good about telling you my secret. I think I feel so good because I am not trying to hide anything anymore. There is something freeing about sharing both the good, deep, beautiful parts *and* the shallow, selfish parts of me with you.

Obviously, I have struggles that are much deeper than my love for *The Bachelor*. I struggle with striving for attention. I often put too much hope in people I date and end up smothering them if I'm not careful. I am not always a good listener. I struggle with being happy in the moment, and I wish for the past or for the future far too often. Sometimes I am terrified of getting older. I can be self-absorbed and selfish at times.

When I focus on these shortcomings, I believe the lie that if people really knew me, they wouldn't like me. To combat this lie, I have to learn to accept myself like God does. The more I accept myself, the more I will be able to accept love from other people. And when I accept myself, I will also be better at loving others in their weakness.

I want to pattern my love for myself, for my potential spouse, for my friends, and for my future children after God's love. God's love is very special. On one hand, he wants us to move from "glory to glory"—to deeper levels of wholeness (2 Corinthians 3:18, KJV). But he also loves us in our imperfections right now, where we are today— whether it is a day in which we are diving into his word at a monastery or a day in which we watch way too many episodes of reality TV.

As Graham Cooke says,

> There is nothing you can do that would make him love you more. There is also nothing you can do to make him love you less. He loves you because he loves you, because he loves you, because he loves you, because that is what he is like [. . . .] It is his nature to love, and you will always be the beloved. He won't love you any better when you become better [. . .] He loves all the way, all the time.[26]

For much of my life I have been scared to show people my imperfections. I often only show the perfect parts of myself. I have hated my imperfections, wondering if those explain why I have been rejected in my life. But now, I want to love myself and others with the kind of love that God loves me with.

Keeping up appearances can be completely exhausting. I don't want to hide "imperfect me" from the world anymore. And even though I consistently want to work to become a more healthy person, I also want to be accepting of today's imperfect me. I am a great big ball of compassion and contemplation and insecurities and *Bachelor* watching and spiritual depth and losing things and quirky humor and deep love for people. I am a mix of good and bad. I am far from perfect. But imperfect me is infinitely valuable and lovable not only to God, but to other people. To myself.

The person whom I may marry one day will also be a ball of wonderful and difficult, just like I am. But I want to love someone like that. I don't want the fairy tale anymore. I want something real. I want someone real.

When I watch *The Bachelor*, I see the flowers and the helicopter rides and the beautiful destinations and the beaches and the bikinis, and I am not in the least bit jealous. I understand that that is not what love is. Romantic love, like the "love" found on *The Bachelor*, is a lot like fireworks, momentarily beautiful but not anything that will last forever. Case in point, only two couples from many many seasons of *The Bachelor* have gotten married. When the fairy tale is no longer staged and the camera stops rolling, there is not a lot of relationship left. It can happen with reality shows, and it can also happen with real-life romances. That is not what I want.

Real love takes hard work. It takes years and even decades of striving to understand and accept who someone is, imperfections and all. Real relationships are made up of hundreds of hours of building a history with someone. If you get married someday, you will not just be married to the person, you will be married to the history that you have built with that person.

As Henri Nouwen says,

> Marriage is not a lifelong attraction of two individuals to each other, but a call for two people to witness together to God's love. The basis of marriage is not mutual affection, or feelings, or emotions and passions that we associate with love, but a vocation, *a being elected to build together a house for God in this world*, to be like the two cherubs whose outstretched wings sheltered the Ark of the Covenant and created a space where Yahweh could be present.[27]

Those are wise words about marriage. Especially from a priest. Do you see now why he is my soul mate?

If I do get married, my husband will love me more than he loves anyone else in the world. He will also probably hurt me more than anyone else in the world will hurt me. I will think there is no one as wonderful as him anywhere. I will also think that there is no one as annoying as him. My job will not be to judge if he is good enough for me. My job will be to love him well. We will build a history together. We will build together a house for God in this world.

Thomas Merton said, "The beginning of love is to let those we love be perfectly themselves, and not to twist them to fit our own image. Otherwise, we love only the reflection of ourselves we find in them."[28]

At this point, I haven't just given up on *meeting* a perfectly-chested bachelor. I've given up on *wanting* anyone who is perfect. I want a real, breathing person. I don't want someone who is ideal, just someone who is a deal. OK, I know. That last line was a bit cheesy. But it might very well make a lot of money as a magnet sold at marriage conferences.

If I get married, my spouse will be real, and he will be hard to live with at times. But that is OK because I will be real, too, and I will be hard to live with at times, too. When I don't expect my mate to be ideal, I won't expect myself to be ideal. I will feel more free to be the imperfect me. I won't need to hide anymore. I won't need to have secrets. I can confess things and not be afraid that it will make me unlovable.

Even now, while we are single, it is important to love our friends and family for who they are, not for who we want them to be.

As my friend Brandon says, marriage should not be about finding a perfect person who will meet all of your needs. Marriage should be about creating a room where both of you can be human.

And I wouldn't mind a room in which I am occasionally allowed to watch reality television.

Chapter Seven

The Case for Thankfulness

"If the only prayer you said in your whole life was 'thank you,' that would suffice." ~Meister Eckhart[29]

This morning I rode my bike along the Coal Creek trail, which is about thirty feet from my house. It is the end of September right now and my favorite time of year in Colorado. The weather for my ride was perfect. The air smelled like a mixture of dying leaves and honeysuckle. The sun was lighting up the rusty scenery like an ethereal baptism. I could hear the rush of the creek beside me, and it sounded like hope.

But there were gnats. Lots of lots of gnats. Like, millions of them. I enjoyed the ride until I would hit pockets of the tiny little nuisances. They would smack me in the face like a sultry woman in a bad soap opera.

I kept thinking, Dang it! This ride would be perfect if

it weren't for the gnats. The little insects were all I could think about the whole ride. I even debated in my head why a good God would create such annoying bugs that often ruin my outdoor experiences.

To escape the gnats, I stopped at my "J" tree by the water. The J tree is, as expected, a tree that looks like a J.

I leaned against my tree, away from the gnats, and breathed deep.

It's a funny thing, air. It always surrounds me, but I seldom remember that it's there. I take it for granted. Every once in a while, though, I stop, open up my lungs, and feel the oxygen rushing through my body, giving me life. I stop and I remember this gift that has been given to me every second since I was born. That's what I did this morning.

I started thinking about how good it felt to breathe after a bike ride. How good it felt to be able to ride a bike—let alone one that was given to me for free—and how good it felt to have this breathtaking landscape sitting thirty feet behind my house, waiting for me to explore it. Then I thought about my body, which had been in constant pain and exhaustion only a few years ago when I was sick with Lyme disease. There is no way that I could have ridden a bike in that terrible season. I could barely walk down the street.

The thing I prayed for more than anything else during that time was for my body to be healthy. It was a desperate, hopeless prayer. I honestly didn't think it would ever be answered.

But here I was, sitting on my J tree, breathing deep. I was incredibly healthy with no constant pain in my joints, with no exhaustion, and with a full night's sleep every night for the last week. And I was riding a bike.

I breathed in deep the air of God's goodness.

My prayer for health had been answered in abundance. But with the challenges and the busyness of the days since my healing, I had forgotten that God had answered that prayer. Sitting by the water, breathing in the crisp air, I remembered. And I was thankful.

On my ride back, I smiled more than I've smiled in a long time.

I quickly realized that smiling isn't the best decision when you are surrounded by gnats, and I reminded myself to floss when I got home.

After my bike ride, I was taught another lesson about thankfulness through my hunt for a new tent.

I have been looking for a new tent for a while. My current thirty-two dollar Target tent has a rainfly that looks a little like an Asian hat and barely covers the screened roof. Every time I go camping, I wonder why the weather is always such that I carefully have to direct the puddles on my floor away from the space where I'm sleeping. It probably has less to do with the weather and more to do with my cheapo tent.

I've used that tent for five summers, so I've been looking for a new one for months now. Avoiding hyperthermia may very well be worth spending a few more dollars.

In hot pursuit of my modern tabernacle in the wilderness, I found a tent on Craigslist that was perfect for me. Great reviews, light, waterproof, three seasons, right size. And forty bucks. Score!

I excitedly called the seller. He told me that he had just sold the tent to someone else. I was really disappointed. I started mulling over in my head how much I wanted that tent.

A few hours later, I went to the streets to play music with some friends. I was shivering quite a bit because I had lost my winter coat. My friend said, "I have a coat I can give you! I was going to give it away anyway." I walked with her to her house, and she gave me a perfect, almost-new, expensive North Face ski jacket.

Now, at the end of the day and as I sit in bed writing, can you guess what I am thinking about? I'll give you one hint: it has everything to do with a tent and nothing to do with a coat.

God is probably up there saying, "Hey, Kate! Did you like that really nice North Face coat I got you? You've been praying for that one!"

All I say is, "MAN! I wanted that tent."

Now I let thoughts go even farther down the road of discontent. I think, *I can't believe I didn't get that tent. I'm going to get hypothermia for sure. I would have had perfect camping experiences for the rest of my life if I had only bought that tent.*

I decide to throw a full on pity party, which I often do. I think, *I always come so close to getting something and then have it taken away from me. That's just how my life is. It doesn't just happen with tents; it happens with people, too. Either they leave me or I lose them.*

And then, the horrible thought crosses my mind that seems to lurk in the corners and pounce when I am not being careful: *I will always be alone.*

This thought startles me. I realize that I went from *I didn't get a forty dollar tent on Craigslist* to *I will always be alone* in the space of a few minutes. How did that happen?

I catch a glimpse of the new coat hanging in the closet, and I recognize my attitude of ungratefulness. Today, I was given the gift of a wonderful bike ride, the remembrance of my health and my dear friends, and a great new coat to keep me warm. But now I can only focus on the tent that I didn't get, which has turned into thinking about the life that I don't have. I realize that I have all but missed the beautiful gifts that God gave me today because I am focusing so much on what he *hasn't* given me.

Someone recently asked me what I would have left if I were to lose everything that I wasn't thankful for today. As I lay here in bed, I think about that, and I am very humbled.

I sit up a little bit. I breathe in. I feel the air rush into my lungs. And I sincerely thank God for the coat. For my bike ride. For my friends. For my health. I don't beg him for the grandiose things he can give me tomorrow. I thank him for the simple things he has already given me today.

That seems to make a way for God to walk into the room. He had been standing nearby the whole time; I just hadn't seen him before. But now I see him. He kisses me on the head.

I look up into his good, good face, and I say, "I'm sorry for forgetting you, Papa."

He says, "That's OK, love. I'm still here."

That is the power of thankfulness. It prepares a way for God to come into the rooms of our hearts so we can look at his good, good face.

We see a dramatic picture of the power of thankfulness in the story of Jehoshaphat, one of the kings of Judah in the Old Testament. He started his reign with great integrity, following in the footsteps of David. The Bible says, "His heart took delight in the ways of the Lord" (2 Chronicles 17:6, NKJV). Jehoshaphat's reign was blessed with God's mercy for a long time.

During this season, God's blessings surrounded Jehoshaphat like air. Often, however, like most of us, he took the air around himself for granted. Jehoshaphat eventually stopped relying on God and started relying on his own ability to control things.

He began to make decisions without God—bad decisions. He decided to align himself with a powerful man named Ahab by arranging the marriage of his own daughter to Ahab's son. Yes, we're talking about Ahab, of Ahab and Jezebel fame. These two are probably the most notoriously evil couple in history.

Not necessarily the smartest choice for in-laws.

The alliance with Ahab soon brought disaster on Jehoshaphat's kingdom, and the king was confronted by the prophet Jehu about his unwise alliance. It was clear that King Jehoshaphat was nowhere near a place of delighting in the Lord anymore. He had stopped trusting in the Lord and had started trusting in his own political decisions. The near demise of his kingdom proved that that was a bad move.

Soon Judah's enemies, the Moabites, formed a powerful confederacy with the surrounding nations, and they planned to attack Jehoshaphat and his people. The enemy army was vast, and the people of Judah were terrified.

People from every region in Judah assembled together to seek the Lord and hear Jehoshaphat's plan: "All the men of Judah, with their wives and children and little ones, stood there before the Lord" (2 Chronicles 20:13, NIV).

I want you to picture this scene for a moment. Jehoshaphat stands before all the people he rules over. He sees husbands and wives together with babies in their arms and toddlers at their feet. Perhaps Jehoshaphat realizes that every person in front of him could potentially be killed because of his decision to control things rather than to trust in God. And now here they are, humbly praying with their king, looking to him for the decision that will determine if they live or die. He wants to make the right decision this time. He doesn't want these people to be destroyed.

So he lays down his manipulative ways, and he puts the future of his kingdom into God's hands.

He does not give the common battle speech: "Boys, we're going to get in there and we are going to destroy them!" Instead, he speaks honest words of desperation. He admits how weak they are. He says, "O, our God [. . .] we have no power to face this vast army that is attacking us. We do not know what to do; but our eyes are upon you" (2 Chronicles 20:12, NIV).

A messenger of the Lord comes and says, "Thus says the Lord to you: 'Do not be afraid nor dismayed because of this great multitude, for the battle is not yours, but God's.'" And then he says, emphasis mine here—"*You will not need to fight in this battle. Position yourselves, stand still* and see the salvation of the Lord, who is with you'" (2 Chronicles 20:15, 17, NKJV).

Listen close, dear readers, because this is, in my opinion, the most important part of the story.

In the morning, as they went out to battle, "Jehoshaphat appointed men to sing to the Lord and to praise him for the splendor of his holiness as they went out at the head of the army, saying: 'Give thanks to the Lord, for his love endures forever'" (2 Chronicles 20:21, NIV).

Consider what a ridiculous war tactic this would seem to be to the men in the army. They have come to fight a battle. Their lives are at stake. Their family's lives are at stake. Their wives may become widows after this day. Their children may become fatherless.

But they have sought the Lord together with their king. Their eyes are set on the Lord alongside their leader. So when Jehoshaphat appoints a worship team to march at the very front of the battle line, ahead of all the strong warriors, they do it. When he asks them to use songs of thankfulness to battle with instead of swords, they go out there and sing with all of their might.

This seems foolish. Did they really think that mere words, a mere attitude of the heart, was going to win a battle for them?

And yet, that is exactly what happened. As the army marched forward praising God, the Moabites that were still far off started quarreling among themselves and ended up killing *each other* before Jehoshaphat's army even got there. Jehoshaphat's army didn't raise one sword. They didn't need to, because they lifted their praises instead.

Perhaps the Moabite army heard the praises of the people and got confused. The enemies were probably asking themselves, "How could they be praising God when they have so little hope that they are going to survive? Maybe there is something that we don't know! Maybe they are more powerful than we think they are!" Fear and chaos ensued.

The truth is, Jehoshaphat's army was thanking God *in spite* of their dire circumstances, and that is what ended up rescuing them. God said that they wouldn't have to fight this battle, and they didn't. Their thankfulness fought the battle for them.

I really love this story because it illustrates that the sword does not always win the battle but that gratefulness often does. Jehoshaphat was wise enough to put the worshippers in front of the army for that reason.

He did not wait for victory to be thankful. His thankfulness is what brought the victory.

Likewise, the enemy is often not defeated by us battling with him, but he is often confused and defeated by thankfulness.

There are times when I don't think I have any strength left in me to battle the loneliness of being single. There are times when I don't think I can make it through another day facing the thought that I might not ever have a biological child. There are times when I'm not sure if I can get through another night of slipping into my single bed alone. There are times when, like Jehoshaphat, I say in desperation, "I have no power to face this vast army that is attacking me! I do not know what to do!" But then I try to gather enough strength and wisdom to add, "but my eyes are on you."

Maybe I would be wise to choose, like Jehoshaphat chose, to fight the battle with the words: "Give thanks to the Lord, for his love endures forever."

When I choose to battle all the plaguing thoughts of loneliness with thankfulness, maybe I will hear the words of my Savior, like Jehoshaphat heard, "You do not need to fight this battle alone, Katie Girl. Stand still. See the salvation of your Lord. I'm still here."

I have been trying to deal with my discontent lately by waking up and saying these simple words over and over again: "Acceptance and gratefulness. Acceptance and gratefulness. Acceptance and gratefulness." Repeating this helps me drown out the mantra that I am more tempted to repeat: "Complaining and bitterness. Complaining and bitterness. Complaining and bitterness." I try to remember that the word "complain" comes from the same root word as "plaintiff," meaning "someone who accuses." In fact, plaintiffs are also called complainants. By complaining, I am accusing God.

I don't want to do that. I want to be grateful. This is the day God has given me. Some of the hours are going to be hard, and some of them are going to be beautiful. It would be wise to accept my reality, whatever that may be, and live as fully as I can within that reality. Rather than waking up and saying "How could this possibly be my life?" I want to be able to say, "This is the day that the Lord has made. Let us rejoice and be glad in it!" (Psalm 118:24, NIV).

When I thank God for this day that he has given me, no matter how difficult it is, my heart will be freed up to behold God's abounding goodness that surrounds me like air every day of my life. I will have serenity not because of my circumstances, but because of my thankfulness.

The power of thankfulness is so strong that it will go

beyond helping me have a good day. It will help me have a good life. When I live my life with acceptance and gratefulness, many of the wounds that I now bear will one day be scars gilded with gold. They will become scars that are beautiful and transforming.

To remind me of this truth, I have a vase full of stones that sits at my bedside. On every stone, I have affixed a picture. For every season of my life, I have one stone with a picture on it that represents the season, and another stone and picture that represents what God taught me in that season.

During the depression I went through in college, symbolized by a picture of a girl crying, I learned that God would heal and restore me as many times as waves crashed to the shore, shown by a picture of a lighthouse.

During the season of my sickness, marked with a picture of a tick, I understood more what it meant to be loved and to depend on those that I love, represented with a picture of a girl holding a heart balloon.

After writing a letter extending forgiveness to someone who greatly hurt me, symbolized by a picture of a letter in a mailbox, I learned that God's forgiveness of me and my forgiveness of others puts me in a place where I can't be bound up by anything, which is represented by a picture of a girl with long red hair dancing with abandon.

I made these stones to be my *ebenezers*, which, literally translated, means "stone of help" (1 Samuel 7:12, NLT). Ebenezer was the site in which the Israelites got the Ark of the Covenant back years after it was stolen from them. Samuel set up a stone memorial in that place and said, "Thus far, the Lord has helped us" (1 Samuel 7:12, NIV).

He set it up as a way to pause and say, "God we have been through a lot, but you have always been faithful. You have helped us before, and you will keep on helping us. Thank you for what you've done so far, and thank you for what you will keep on doing."

I look through my stones occasionally to remember that God has helped me through every season of my life. They bring me a great sense of gratitude for all that God has done for me in my life.

These stones mark the trials of my life, but they also mark the wisdom gained, the life lived, and the trust for the one who never stops walking with me. If I keep walking this road with God, the hard trial I endure now will one day be a picture on a stone, marking the wisdom that God gave me in this part of my journey.

I will look at that stone, and I will be grateful for this season, no matter how hard it was in the moment. That stone will help me remember that no matter what I go through in life, "God causes all things to work together for good to those who love God, to those that are called according to his purpose" (Romans 8:28, NAS).

As Jean Baptiste of Massieu said, "Gratitude is a memory of the heart."

I remember today, God. I remember.

Chapter Eight

The Great Name Changer

I am many things other than a single woman: lover of God, lover of people, traveler of the world, teacher, lover of the poor and downcast, avid reader, overcomer of a chronic disease, ridiculous enjoyer of dark chocolate and good cheese, lover of nature, worshipper. But "single" is often the only label I give myself.

The labels you give yourself and that others give you slowly build a path that you will likely end up following, like water in the crevice of a rock. Unless you consciously direct the water somewhere else by believing what God says about you, you will often flow wherever that label wants to take you.

For instance, constantly comparing yourself to magazine models might give you the idea that you are ugly. Believing that label could you lead you down the road of low self-worth and eating disorders. If you grow up with a father who tells you that you will never amount to anything, you may call yourself failure and never attempt to get an education or a good job. If several people have broken up with you or have cheated on you, you may label yourself as unlovable and, consequently, you may shy away from getting close to people so they won't reject you.

You will live out these labels unless you consciously replace them with your true identity. In the above cases, you could say, "I am not ugly; I am beautiful," "Failure is not my destiny; abundance is," or, "I am not unlovable; the more people get to know me, the more they love me." Regularly replacing the lies with the truth is crucial to living a life that is not determined by your past.

There is a favorite story of mine that I want to share here that beautifully illustrates a group of people replacing an inaccurate label with their true identity.

A group of Latino immigrants lived in an apartment complex in the Westlake area of Los Angeles. The Latino tenants were labeled as "poor" and perhaps even "worthless" and so they were treated that way by their slum landlords. The living conditions were awful. The *Los Angeles Times* said that the apartments were one of the "worse slum disgraces in the city."[30] Cockroaches infested everything. The lights and showers often didn't work, the toilets were clogged, and there was a lake of sewage in the basement. Up to that point the tenants hadn't challenged their landlord's ill-treatment of them. Perhaps they didn't believe they deserved any better. Soon there were open drug deals, shootings, and stabbings occurring inside the apartments.

A group of InnerCHANGE missionaries decided to live out the Gospel by moving into these horrible living conditions and loving their new neighbors well. The missionaries slowly became a trusted part of the community. Some of the tenants and missionaries had such a strong connection that they considered each other family. The InnerCHANGE team helped the Latino immigrants remember that they were not merely poor; in God's eyes they were precious.

After a season, a group of the Latino tenants created a task force attempting to change their horrible living conditions. They met in the InnerCHANGE apartments because they knew the missionaries would help guide them in their efforts.

Three Latino women, named Teresa, Josefina, and Maria, became passionate about advocating for their cause. The InnerCHANGE team supported them, but they did not take over. Together, they organized legal action against the owners of the apartment building. It took six years of fighting together, but all of the tenants eventually became co-op owners of the building. In the history of Los Angeles, that had never happened before.

Toward the end of the effort to reclaim their homes, one of the men who lived in the complex was diagnosed with inoperable cancer. He held on long enough to walk with his family through the doors of his newly owned apartment, and he was so proud. It was the first time he had ever owned a home. Two days after moving in, he died. The tenants went door-to-door to collect money for the family. This simple act illustrated that this place that used to be filled with prejudice and murder was now a community.

Teresa, Josefina, and Maria have been given many

awards, and they have even been flown to conferences to talk how about how to bring dignity and justice to poor communities. One by one, these brave women are helping other poor people rise above their physical and emotional poverty.

My point in telling this story is to illustrate that there is incredible power in rising above your labels. This community went from believing they were worthless to believing they were valuable, from being poor to being homeowners, from being violent to being family. They were encouraged to believe in their true identity and throw out the labels people had put on them, and they did.[31]

We see from this story that *who you believe you are changes everything.*

The biblical story of Jacob illustrates this same idea— that you often become what you label yourself.

In Hebrew culture, the firstborn son was given two different endowments: a birthright, which allowed him to take on his father's name in social and legal matters, and a double portion of the inheritance. The firstborn was a coveted position, and there is no clearer example of a man who coveted this position than Jacob.[32]

Jacob came out of the womb with his hand outstretched, grasping his twin brother Esau's heal, desperate to win in the race for firstborn. It seems that even in the first seconds of his life, Jacob was trying to control his own destiny. He was given the name Jacob, a name that means "deceiver," or "supplanter," which could also be interpreted as "one who wants be what he is not."

Sound familiar?

Not surprisingly, the one who was given the name

"deceiver" became one of the most notorious deceivers in the Bible. For most of his life, Jacob tried to reverse that he was born only seconds after his brother. His life was defined by this perceived injustice.

To put it bluntly, Jacob wanted to be someone else so much that he became a control freak.

Here are some examples. When Esau came in starving after hunting, Jacob offered food in exchange for his birthright. Later, Jacob pretended to be Esau when his father Isaac was dying so that his father would give him the father's blessing, which would in turn give Jacob a double portion of the inheritance as if he were the firstborn.

Jacob wasn't firstborn, but, by God, he knew he was *supposed* to be firstborn. Maybe if he worked really hard at it, if he spent his life trying to change it, he could trick himself, his family, and even his God into believing that he was firstborn. The ironic thing is that it was prophesied from birth that "the elder would serve the younger." (Genesis 25:25, KJV.) All of this manipulation was for naught, as Jacob would have eventually been the one in authority even without his control-freakish ways.

My trials look different than Jacob's looked. Jacob rehearsed over and over in his head that if he had been the firstborn he would have had all that he wanted. I rehearse over and over in my head that if God would give me a husband that adores me, I would have all that I want. If I had children who loved the Lord, I would have all that I want. If my career worked out and people around the world listened to my music and read this book, I would have all that I want. If my relationships did not fail and I were never rejected, I would have all that I want.

I, too, want to be someone I am not. I know that God understands this struggle, but I also know he doesn't want me to constantly mull over how unsatisfied I am with my life. He knows that when I do that, I am living as "one who wants to be who she is not."

I, like Jacob, often want God's promises sooner than he has given them to me. I want my right to marry, and I throw caution to the wind and say, "By God, I'm going to get it." But the truth is, if I try to manipulate God's promise, the fruit will be slavery rather than freedom. If I refuse God's help and try to do it on my own, if I become obsessed with figuring out how to get what I want when I want it, I will become a slave to my desires. I will sacrifice my peace for my expectations.

These control-freak tendencies can even look like godly practices sometimes. Maybe if I pray enough? Fast enough? If I let go enough? These actions turn into slavery if my motivation is to get what I want rather than to get closer to God.

I mourn when I think about how I've treated God at times. This is my Jesus, who feels deeper and loves more passionately than anyone in the world. This is the one who has journeyed with me, who has comforted me, and who has been faithful to me every second of my life. This is the one who bled and died so that he could be near me when I ache for a husband.

And now, in my pain, I often reduce him to a genie in a bottle who grants me wishes if I rub the right way.

Forgive me, Lord, forgive me.

After Jacob stole the birthright and the father's blessing from his older brother, he married and lived many years in prosperity. One year, Jacob traveled with his family to Canaan. He heard news that Esau, whom he hadn't seen since Jacob swindled him, was coming to meet him with an army of four hundred men. Terrified, he sent gifts to Esau, hoping to ease the wrath his brother might bring against him.

That same night, he took his family to cross a river called Jabbok. Jabbok means "a place of emptying out," or "a place of passing over," and was a symbol of struggle to the Hebrew people.[33] Jacob sent his wives and possessions over across the river and was left alone. What an incredible picture! The things he had fought so hard for—his inheritance and his family—were the things he needed to let go of in order to find his true identity.

As he watched the dreams he based his identity on fade away in the distance, he stood alone on the other side, stripped down to barest part of who he was. That night, Jacob had a strange experience with a "man" who Jacob later identified as God:

> So Jacob was left alone, and a man wrestled with him till daybreak. When the man saw that he could not overpower him, he touched the socket of Jacob's hip so that his hip was wrenched as he wrestled with the man (Genesis 32:24, NIV).

Like Jacob, I have come to a turning point where I know I can't control my circumstances. I am learning that I can't manipulate my way into getting God's promise. What I can do, though, is to try to find God in the midst of my circumstances. God has come to wrestle with me. And after all these years, I have learned this: I would rather wrestle with God than try to control my circumstances and be called "the one who wants to be what she is not."

I want to see the real God, not some version I create of him that suits all of my needs. Like C.S. Lewis wrote while reflecting on the death of his wife,

> My idea of God is not a divine idea. It has to be shattered time after time. He shatters it himself. He is the great iconoclast [someone who shatters false idols, religious images, settled beliefs and institutions]. Could we not say that this shattering is one of the marks of his presence?[34]

I want to wrestle with God like Jacob did. I want to ask him the hard questions that don't make any sense. I want to come to him as lovers might come together, quarreling so that they will ultimately understand each other more. To look at each other face-to-face and to be brutally honest, not for the sake of being right but for the sake of being intimate.

Because he is the great iconoclast, he might shatter my image of him. When I wrestle him, he will be more mind-boggling and infinitely bigger than the box I have put him in. He will break down who I thought he was and the borders I have forced him into, like a street performer that contorts his body to fit it into a little box. Then perhaps I will accept him for all that he is, even the parts that I don't understand. He will transform the way that I see him, and, thus, he will transform the way that I see myself.

Jacob's story goes on:

> Then the man said, "Let me go, for it is daybreak."
>
> But Jacob replied, "I will not let you go unless you bless me."
>
> The man asked him, "What is your name?"
>
> "Jacob," he answered.
>
> Then the man said, "Your name will no longer be Jacob, but Israel, because you have struggled with God and with men and have overcome."
>
> Jacob called the place Peniel [which means "Face of God"] saying, "It is because I saw God face-to-face, and yet my life was spared" (Genesis 32:26-30, NIV).

At the end of their wrestling, Jacob asked for a blessing. God could have offered Jacob many things for this blessing—more wealth, more fame, more wives. But God offered none of these things because he knew there was one thing that Jacob wanted more than anything else, and that was what God wanted to give him.

He offered Jacob a new name.

Jacob took that offer gladly. After being called "deceiver"

every day of his life, he was ready for a new identity.

God changed Jacob's name to Israel. Israel means "one who wrestles with God." God said he gave him this name because Jacob "struggled with God and man and overcame" (Genesis 32:28, NIV). He was now named "overcomer."

Overcomer became Jacob's new identity. He was no longer deceiver. God changed his name, and that changed everything.

Jacob's new name, Israel, was the name that was given as an inheritance to his descendants. It is the name that is still used today for the chosen people, a people that we as the body of Christ have been grafted into. We are no longer called manipulators or supplanters. We are the ones who have wrestled with God and have come out changed. The ones who have met him face-to-face.

Revelation 2:17 says, "To him who overcomes, I will give him some of the hidden manna. I will also give him a white stone with a new name written on it, known only by him who receives it" (NIV).

This verse closely parallels the story of Jacob. A new name will be given to him who overcomes, to him who wrestles. The new name is so intimate; it is something that is only between you and God.

What is the name that God has given you? What is the name that will overcome your insecurities, the lies you have been told? Take a moment and ask God what this new name, this new identity is for you.

I want to wrestle with God, even it is difficult. I want my new name, my new identity. When I wrestle him, he will tell me to ask the hard questions. He might not give me the answers I want. He might not give me any answers.

But it is his choice. He is God.

In the end, I know that I want a God who is free, not a God who answers when I pray as if prayers are like spells I can cast on my life by saying the right words. I don't want a God like the millions of trinket-gods on street corners around the world that can be bribed with offerings. I want a God who is bigger than me, who is stronger than me, and who comes down and wrestles with me so that we can be close.

And after my wrestling, I may walk away with a limp like Jacob did. But receiving a limp is better than pushing God away. For in my wrestling, I touch God. I touch the God who speaks a word and stars and moon and universe are made. I touch the God who opens his heart and all things tender and all things passionate and all things beautiful flow out like water. That is the God I wrestle with. He and I will touch and sometimes it will hurt, but I will come away changed. I will not leave with the answers to all my questions, but I will have seen the face of God. And I will see love in his eyes.

Maybe my name will be changed like Jacob's was. Maybe I will no longer simply name myself "single," because I will have seen his eyes and I will know the truth:

I am named Beloved.

What names do you give yourself? What names do other people give you? Divorced? Poor? Abandoned? Sick? Widowed? Fatherless? Failure?

Not anymore. Wrestle with your God and know the truth. You are his beloved.

How to Communicate

1.) Show up.
2.) Tell your truth.
3.) Trust God.
4.) Let go of the outcome.

Chapter Nine

What Single People Wish Married People Knew

My child,

I watched you as you were sleeping last night. I spilled moon-light over you and kissed your cheek.

I saw that you were crying. You were crying out for that one whom you have always longed for. The one whom I have created you for.

Oh precious one, I tell you this: when you can trust me completely, when you can let go of your dreams of a spouse and give your desires to me, that's when I will bring you the love of your life.

I am forever yours,

Jesus

I remember reading a letter like this as a handout in my Christian campus group when I was in college. It was a very popular letter back then.

The font: calligraphy that looked like real handwriting. The sentiment in the room: tender. The result: aforementioned letter hung from yellow thumbtacks on the walls of thousands of dorm rooms.

The theology created around this letter and similar bad sermons and books: total crap.

I assure you, many a Christian female read that letter, grabbed their Bibles and journals, went to a quiet place, turned their sweet young faces toward heaven with tears in their eyes and said, "Lord, I let go. I give my husband to you."

Do you know why? Because those women wanted a husband, and according to the letter, if you want a husband you let go of him first. So they let go of him in order to get him.

Quite ironic, isn't it?

Some of those lovely young coeds got older and didn't get married, not even after many teary sessions of letting go. Gradually, their prayers went from a very serene, very quiet, "I let go" to a "Do you hear me, God?! I let go! I let go! I let go!" with their hands pumping the air.

Doesn't really sound like a peaceful place, does it? Then again, David doesn't sound very peaceful when he says, "How long, O Lord? Will you forget me forever? How long will you hide your face from me?" (Psalm 13:1, NIV). David, too, struggled with frustration and longing. He says he watered his pillow with tears (Psalm 6:6).

Of course, David didn't only mourn. There were times that he wildly praised God with everything in him, too.

Then again, so do we.

Sometimes we wake up and are thankful to God. We

trust him. We see the way he has provided for us and the way he makes sense out of a life that doesn't often make sense. We recognize some of the freedom we have as singles and some of the benefits, and we are grateful. We worship with all that we are.

Other times, we hear the nineteenth person that week say something like, "When you least expect to find your spouse, he will come right around the corner."

We suppress the urge to respond, "I definitely gave up expecting it now that I'm over thirty. That formula of yours doesn't seem to be working because I've been least expecting it for two decades, and it still ain't happenin', sista."

Married friends, I want you to know that sometimes we go home after those conversations and weep and gnash our teeth and water our pillows with tears.

Well, maybe it's not that bad, but it's not very fun.

If I mention the topic of this book to single people, I often hear a multitude of frustrations about what well-meaning married people say to them. By far the most common is some version of that same popular formula:

When you let go, Jesus will bring your spouse.

In fact, this particular equation—the when-you-let-go-your-husband-will-come equation—has been the most popular how-to-not-be-single formula in the church for quite a while. It feels like people are saying, "This isn't out of your control! It's something you just bring to the Lord and then everything will be all right. Don't worry, honey. You just get out there and give it to God and your spouse will come." Ugh.

Married couples, church-at-large, I will let you know a

secret right now. Almost every thinking person out there who is single feels offended and hurt when given this little formula.

The truth is, life doesn't work that way. God makes all things right eventually but not often in our timing or in ways that we expect. And most of the time we can't control our circumstances with simple formulas. There are actually very few things in the Bible that are that formulaic. Certain things are black and white, such as the goodness of God, the mandate to worship, etc. But when it comes to characters in the Bible and their stories—well, they are all different. Everyone's journey is unique and has its own challenges and joys.

Before I sound too cynical, I want to give some credit to all the beautiful, caring, married friends out there. My friend Becca mentioned the other day that a lot of married people have a formula mentality because they actually want to help single people. Humans want a nice, neat, black-and-white answer. We don't like things that don't make sense, especially when it comes to people we love. So if someone is single and really struggling with being single, his or her married friends, pastors, and even other single people often hand out formulas like raffle tickets, hoping to help ease the pain.

I know that Becca's right. Married people are not trying to be malicious when they offer the formula; they are trying to be comforting.

But my friends, it's not comforting. It hurts.

We singles really do want to be comforted, but the formula method often comes across as a "just add water" kind of comfort.

Let me give you a little story to illustrate: Picture me at thirty, eating lunch with Emily. She is someone whom I love and respect, and she is someone who had become a leader for me at the time of our lunch date. Keep in mind that she got married at twenty-four (which, she often points out, felt like a lifetime to her because she had been wanting marriage since she was sixteen. That's eight years of waiting, she says. Hmmm, with that math I have been waiting for twenty years). Anyway, at our lunch we talk about dating. I express my frustrations about being single. I am vulnerable enough to tell her that even though I'm trying to trust God, I am really struggling with being alone.

She twirls her angel hair pasta and says, "Kate, do you remember our babysitter, Joann? Well, she also went through a season of really struggling with being single. She cried and battled and finally brought her burden to the Lord. She was able to give up her husband, just like Abraham gave up Isaac. Two weeks later, she met her husband, and he looks just like Ryan Gosling."

"Emily, I am really happy for Joann," I answer. "But she is twenty freaking years old."

"So? What does that have to do with anything?"

Now, in that season of my life, I didn't often stand up to leaders even if I was frustrated. But it was just too much for me this time.

I continue: "I have had a decade longer than her of wrestling with God over this issue. Another decade of waking up alone. Another decade of longing for someone to hold me. In all my wrestling, I have had several seasons where I have been content as a single person, embracing the thought of God as my husband. But often those seasons fade and then I'm struggling again. I don't think God laughs at my cycles of frustration. I think he understands. I think he wants to meet me in them."

Emily keeps arguing with me, saying that I just need to let go and insinuating that my singleness is my own fault.

I finally say, "Em, please understand me here. If you had a friend who was not getting pregnant or who was having multiple miscarriages or someone who had been struggling with barrenness for ten years, would you say to her 'Well, if you just trusted the Lord more with your barrenness, he would give you a baby'? You would never say that! You would recognize how much she mourns the loss, and you would be sensitive in your words. You wouldn't want to hurt her more by making her feel like her struggle might be her own fault. At times I feel barren—not only barren as a mother, but barren as a lover, as well. I don't have children or a husband, and so I really have no immediate blood family. Please, please be sensitive to this barrenness in me. Please don't tell me that I have done something wrong and that the result of my shortcoming is barrenness."

The sad thing is, Emily still didn't get it. She held on to her perception that if I was more consistent in trusting God, he would bring me my man. She had to have another conversation with a single friend of mine before she realized that maybe it wasn't the most sensitive thing in the world to say. She later apologized.

The reason the if-you-just-let-go formula is so frustrating is that it makes us feel like our being single has nothing to do with God's will or our choices or the enemy or any other theory one might have about why difficult things happen. It makes us feel like *our singleness is a result of our lack.*

We already struggle with feeling like we are lacking when we wonder why we haven't been chosen. Please don't cut that wound deeper.

The formula also makes us feel like our not being married has to do with our relationship with the Lord, which, according to the formula, is also lacking.

For most of us singles, our relationship with the Lord is the most sacred relationship we have. Please, please don't criticize that relationship, as well. Don't tear down one of the only relationships in which we feel loved and accepted.

There is a very thick book of popular maxims and theologies that are not actually in the Bible (though many people might think they are). This book, that I like to call *First Assumptions,* is a book in which we have verses like "This too shall pass," "Cleanliness is next to Godliness," "God moves in mysterious ways," and "God helps those who help themselves." Well, in this book there is a chapter of formulas, and in it one can find this lovely one that may very well have come straight from the letter at the beginning of this chapter:

Not letting go = being single.

Letting go = being married.

Here is Emily's contribution to that chapter:

Relinquishing your dreams to the Lord = husband that looks like Ryan Gosling.

Let's explore some other formulas that might be found in that chapter, shall we?

My friend Jess is a very beautiful blond girl who has

been a missionary in Italy for ten years and is the same age as I am. One day an Italian woman, let's call her Mamma Carmen, came up to her with a little charm necklace that had a picture of a saint on it.

"What's this?" asked Jess.

(Cue accent of Italian mama who doesn't speak much English.) "A necklace for-a you. A picture of-a Saint Anthony."

"Who is Saint Anthony?"

"Is-a-the patron saint of lost-a things."

"And what have I lost, Mama Carmen?"

"Oh-a, you know, sveetie."

"No, I don't know. What is that I have lost?"

"You lost-a your husband."

"Mama Carmen, isn't that usually the saint you pray to for a lost sock or car keys—things like that?"

"Yes, but not-a for you. For you, pray to him for husband. More important than sock."

Mama Carmen's formula:

Lost husband + praying to Patron Saint of Lost Things + ten Hail Marys = one wedding, five socks, two spoons, and a bracelet you thought you gave to your friend Jill.

It seems to me that the if-you-just-let-go-your-spouse-will-come formula is much more prevalent in church culture than it is in secular culture. In fact, just the other day I was talking to two single guy friends of mine who are both over thirty. One is very involved in church culture and the other doesn't often go to church. I was telling them how hard it was when people give me "the formula," and my non-church-going friend said, "Wait. You guys have had that said to you?"

"Of course," said my other guy friend, "like every week of my life."

"No one has ever said that to me."

It makes you wonder how many of these formulas come from our church culture and not from the Lord's heart.

When used in the wrong context, these pat answers can be very damaging. Donald Miller said, "As much as we want to believe we can fix our lives in about as many steps as it takes to make a peanut butter sandwich, I don't believe we can."[35]

Here is another example that parallels what I go through as a single. When I was sick, I developed a new respect for people who are chronically ill. It is difficult beyond words to be sick like that. My illness was something that was on my mind almost every minute of the day. It took so much for me to get past my pain and the wall of my exhaustion that it was difficult for me to keep my mind on anything else. Of course, my well-meaning friends and other people at church wanted to comfort me.

On one hand, I appreciated how often people prayed for my healing. On the other hand, I felt very sad when their "comfort" came with a note that characters in the Bible were healed because of their faith, which, of course, communicated to me that if I wasn't getting better, it must have been because I didn't have enough faith. According to this formula, my sickness wasn't going away because I was doing something wrong.

I now see that it took a whole lot of faith for me to get through that sickness still believing that God is good.

It also took a whole lot of faith for my friend Carrie, who battled cancer with incredible composure, to believe in God's goodness. She was healed for a season, praised God, and soon, she got much worse. She died. Does her death mean she didn't have enough faith?

The main speaker at Carrie's funeral was a co-worker who was also an atheist. He said that he had never met anyone who loved God like Carrie did. He said that even when her body dwindled away and was ravished by disease, her face would light up when she talked about Jesus. She was not bitter toward God. Instead, she knew God was her hope. At the end of his speech he said, "I know Carrie is in the arms of Jesus somewhere now, so grateful to finally be with him." This was from an atheist. Everyone in the room was crying.

If that is not faith, I don't know what is. Sometimes bad things happen and there is no formula or pat answer to explain why they do.

All of this talk reminds me of the story of Job. You probably know this one. A good guy gets pummeled by dying kids and ruined houses and horrible boils. His friends come in and tell him their theories about why he is suffering. They give him all kinds of formulas. Most of the formulas have to do with how Job must have had some hidden sin or was doing something wrong.

Here is the formula we could come up with from Job's story:

Tragically losing everything + wife that is pissed + hideous boils all over your body + annoying friends telling you that you must have done something wrong to deserve this + being totally frustrated and not understanding + God's booming voice telling you that you don't know as much as you think you do and that he doesn't fit into formulas and boxes + praising God even through horrible circumstances and singing "Blessed Be Your Name" = twice as much stuff than you had before.

This story clearly articulates that formulas do not explain away difficult circumstances.

On top of creating formulas that we think are biblical, we tend to create our own formulas based on our experiences. It is easy to sum up our experiences into pat stories that make everyone else feel like relationships and marriage should look a certain way. Through these new made-up formulas, we try and tell each other why a relationship does or doesn't, or should or shouldn't, happen.

Here is an example:

My husband and I met in the grocery store aisle, so go put on your cutest sundress, grab some strawberries, and then nonchalantly drop the strawberries in front of that cute guy in the produce section.

Another example is if a single person has gone through a bad breakup, a married person will often use their own experience as a formula to make the unmarried person feel like it might still work out.

We had been broken up for two years. I was on a date with someone else, and he came in with an engagement ring and said that he realized he couldn't live without me. We've been married eight years now.

The motivation of the married person here is not to give false hope. He or she just wants to make an uncontrollable situation seem more controllable. But you know what? These formulas often do give us false hope.

If a married (or divorced) person has gone through something really hard, he or she will often make a formula out of that, as well. I have heard both of these:

Don't ever ever ever marry your best friend. It will never work out.

and

Don't ever ever ever marry someone who is not your best friend. It will never work out.

Married people, pastors, ministry leaders, you need to realize that when single people like me are in a season of loneliness, we often cling to the formulas that you give us. We will put makeup on to go to the grocery store to get strawberries and drop them like they're hot because someone once said that is a good way to get husbands.

When there has been a breakup, our instinct to cling to formulas happens even more frequently and can be even more detrimental. The story about the proposal from the guy two years after the couple broke up? I have thought of that story many times after my own breakups.

It's not that I don't want to hear your story. I love hearing people's stories. Sometimes the stories have given me hope. But other times, when your story turns into a black-and-white formula, the advice can become unhealthy. If I cling to that breakup story when I am lonely and I want my boyfriend back, I need to step back and take caution. All of our stories are very different, and both married people and singles need to remember that.

I think a good rule of thumb is to do less formula making and pat-answering and to do more listening. Listening and loving are so closely related that sometimes it's hard to tell the difference. Listen to what the Lord has to say and listen to what the one who is struggling has to say. We singles might ask you for formulas—even beg you for formulas—because we want you to be able to help us fix things. But for the most part, those formulas don't help.

I don't want to make it sound like you shouldn't feel free to share your own experience as a married person, but I also want to make it very clear that everyone's journey is different. Try not to let your own emotions, your own hopes, and your own frustrations go into your advice giving. Try to restrain yourself from giving out formulas.

But never restrain yourself from giving us a hug. We probably really need one.

And singles, maybe we should stop clinging to formulas like dryer sheets cling to clothes. Maybe we need to realize that we have our own journeys, and all of our journeys are valid.

Chapter Ten

What Married People Wish Single People Knew

My brother Will and my sister-in-law Marie had twins last October. The twins were 8 lb. 10 oz. and 7 lb. 7 oz. That's sixteen pounds of baby inside another human being.

Toward the end of her pregnancy, Marie grew weary of people saying, "You look like you are about to burst!" or "You're as big as a house!" Her belly might not have been as big as a house, but it certainly was as big as a suburban condo. A very attractive, feisty, hippie, suburban condo, might I add.

Will and Marie also have a beautiful four-year-old with cerebral palsy named John Mark. He is one of the loves of my life. Because John Mark can't walk, they have had three non-walking children for over a year since the birth of the twins. When Will takes the kids out, he straps one twin into a carrier on his front, he straps one onto his back, and then he sets John Mark in a stroller. Watching

Will cart around three babies is as fascinating to watch as it is to watch a woman in Africa putting forty-eight pounds of water on her head.

The twins are now a year and a half old, and I recently visited their family for Christmas. Will and I put on a puppet show on Christmas morning complete with a spontaneous song called "No Tacos for Christmas" that we performed with Latino accents. The three kids sat on chairs in front of the homemade puppet theatre and belly laughed for a full hour.

It is during moments like those that I ache for children of my own.

A day or so after the puppet show, we went to the dentist's office. Marie asked me to watch the twins for about ten minutes while she got her teeth cleaned. I had worked at a daycare for five years, so I didn't think that watching them would be very difficult.

I was wrong.

Jeremiah crawls crazy fast. I think he could beat most Olympians.

His speed made my time at the dentist's office difficult to say the least. When I held Arowyn, Jeremiah crawled down the hallway at record speeds, straight toward the dentist's not-child-proofed drills. When I set Arowyn down to grab her brother, she went speeding down the hallway toward that fun buzzing noise, which was actually someone getting a root canal. Surely a root canal is not a procedure during which a dentist would want an adorable toddler under his feet.

I spent those minutes running down the hallway, picking one baby up and plopping it down in the waiting room, and then running down the hallway again, picking the other baby up and plopping that one down in the waiting room. This went on for what seemed like forever. Within minutes, I was frazzled. I was perplexed as to how Will and Marie could do this for fourteen hours a day.

Will and Marie barely ever complain about their kids. When asked, they don't go on a tyrannical rampage explaining how having twins is harder than surviving the Bubonic plague. (I have heard other people make this analogy about their twins.) In fact, Will and Marie often refer to their children as the most important blessing of their lives. There is power in speaking blessing, even when a child can't understand those words. Will and Marie are also super-humanly patient when their children are screaming louder than a bad emo band for nine hours straight.

Do you remember how, in the introduction to this book, I said that I understand that having a family is difficult? After I spend time with Will and Marie and their kids, I realize one important thing:

I. Do. Not. Get. It.

I don't understand what it is like to live day-to-day with someone, with their weaknesses exposed for me to see on a regular basis. I don't understand what it is like to have children vying for my attention every hour of the day, like Will and Marie do. I can't understand it because I haven't experienced it.

Let me add something here. I do struggle with people telling me how hard marriage is, which is the default response when people find out that I am in my thirties and not married. They often feel like it is their duty to warn me of the impending doom that will be mine if I choose matrimony as my life sentence.

I usually get very defensive when this happens, thinking, *My life can be hard, too! I would give up a lot to have someone choose me. To have children.* But lately, after seeing more and more friends divorce, I have been thinking it might be wiser for me to listen than to get angry. The truth is, people like Will and Marie have experience that I don't have. I should discipline the bratty children named Ego and Arrogance inside my head. I should take to heart the advice of my married friends and learn something that will help me love better whether I get married or not. Thus, I have decided to interview several couples and several divorced people for this book, and I have asked them to share their advice for us single people.

"Oh no!" I'm sure you are yelling right about now. "I trusted you, Kate. Yours is the first book I have read in a long time that has not told me in the first few sentences that I am required to appreciate my gift of singleness. How could you make me sit through married-people advice?"

Calm yourself. The following points were said so many times by the people I interviewed that I think they are worth listening to. Paying attention here could save us many years of heartache, and it could greatly benefit the relationships we have now, too.

Take a deep breath. Let's walk through this together. We will be all right. And it will be worth it. Here is the advice that was mentioned the most from my interviewees:

1.) Get as healthy as possible while you are single.

During your single years, your dysfunction mostly affects you and your own life. When you are married, your dysfunction deeply affects the closest people in your lives and can potentially really hurt them. My spiritual mom told me this years ago, and her advice was one of the reasons that I started going to see a counselor. I wanted to be a healthier person, both to honor myself and to honor the family I may have one day.

Some people think that only crazies get counseling. But I have come to believe that people who invest in their own emotional well-being are the healthiest people I know because they actually work to get better. People who have huge splinters of wood buried in them are not healthy. They might seem healthy, but there is probably an infection under the surface. People who want to be healthy realize that they have some issues and goes to a professional to get those splinters of wood removed.

I am a frugal person, but I have learned that my emotional and physical health are two things I shouldn't scrimp on. It is invaluable to work with a professional in order to live a better life. Spending money on counseling is, hands down, the best money I have ever spent.

It is important to look for an amazing person whom we want to spend the rest of our lives with, but it just as important to *become* an amazing person. Working on our emotional well-being through counseling is an important way to do this. Furthermore, if we work on our emotional well-being, I bet that we will find out that we attract people who are at the same level of health that we are. The healthier we are, the more likely we are to attract people who are also healthy. But let's not work on ourselves just to attract people. Let's work on ourselves because we deserve to be healthy.

Truly, being emotionally stable is way more fun than being a basket case. Take it from me. I've been both.

In addition to going to counseling as a single person, I think we'd be wise to also consider going to counseling once we start seriously dating someone. Although it sounds foreign to go to "dater's counseling," doing so makes sense. Either the counseling will help a couple see that they are not a good match or it will help build a good foundation for the future marriage. Invaluable and worth every penny.

2.) Be careful with your expectations of marriage.

Re-read my chapter on expectations. Then re-read it again. Then ponder if re-reading what you re-read means that you re-re-read it. Then be reminded of this important point: It will save you immeasurable amounts of disappointment to work now on having realistic expectations about marriage. This was the advice most emphasized to me by my married friends.

As I mentioned in the previous chapter, if your expectations are too high going into a marriage, you can end up resenting the person you marry simply because that person is not fulfilling your life the way you wanted.

The more we keep our expectations in check now, the easier it will be for us to keep our expectations in check when we are married. If we can foresee that false expectations are a dangerous road to go down, we will not put as much pressure on our spouse to give us happiness if we do get married.

3.) Recognize how weighty the decision to marry is. Decide with both your heart and your head whether or not it is a wise choice to marry the person you are dating.

It's true: deciding who we marry is probably the most important decision of our lives. It will affect everything. Both married and divorced people I interviewed stressed this point again and again, especially if they made hasty decisions that they regretted later.

Turns out, most people don't have the best judgement when first in love. There is a good reason for this: most of them are basically thinking like drug addicts. Seriously. According to the National Public Radio show *Radiolab*, in an episode called, "This is Your Brain on Love," scientists have looked at the brains of people who are newly in love and compared them to the brains of cocaine addicts. They looked very similar.

According to the radio program, there are many naturally occurring chemicals we become addicted to when we fall in love. The most prominent one is dopamine. This is a chemical that makes a person feel happy and passionate. When first attracted to someone, a person has huge surges of dopamine running through his or her body.

If dopamine were a woman at a party she would be the one who is a really good kisser and who looks amazing in her skin-tight outfit but who really doesn't want anything long-term. She comes on strong and it feels really good to be around her, but her commitment quickly fades. Her love is not the kind of love that is sustainable.

Thankfully, after six months or so of being in a relationship with someone, a hormone called oxytocin comes into the mix that starts displacing the dopamine. This chemical is marked with a sense of calm and stability rather than with unsustainable highs. It lasts much longer than dopamine, even if it doesn't make a person as "happy." It helps one person attach to another, and it promotes contentment in that relationship.

Oxytocin is comparable to that really nice girl next door with a southern accent. The one who is not as flashy but who has a good heart and who would probably make a really good wife some day.[36]

Our Hollywood-saturated society often gives us the idea that love is simply having the feeling that dopamine running through our system gives us. But chemicals that make us happy and uncontrollably passionate are not what make love last. They may help draw us to someone, but they don't foster long-term commitment. Once we are committed to our mate, dopamine will help bring a little romance, but it is not the glue that holds a marriage together. It is sobering to see how many divorces and affairs have happened because people have mistaken this chemically-induced feeling for love and have abandoned their partner when the "love" wears off.

Interesting, isn't it? Perhaps we should keep this theory in mind as we date. Perhaps we should remember that our brains are a bowl of hormonal soup right now. And bowls of hormonal soup do not often make good decisions.

Let's let ourselves be in love. Let's be aware and appreciative of this special season during which it feels so good to be in someone's presence. Let's let dopamine do its job and let it attract us to someone who could be a good partner. But let's not put dopamine in the driver's seat and propel us to make big decisions unwisely.

Clearly, we will need to give ourselves time while we are dating to let some of these chemicals wear off so we can be sober in our decision making. Romance and the feeling of being high on love won't guarantee a good marriage. Rather than relying solely on our feelings to make decisions, we should be sure to ask lots of practical questions over time about the person we are dating. Does this person have a good track record in how he or she has treated me? Do I keep telling myself that he has good potential? That she will get better with time? Getting married to someone who has a good track record is a pretty safe choice. Marrying someone who just has potential is not very safe. And track records take time.

There is great wisdom in looking for the fruit of something even when it is still a seed. Yes, you might be in love now, but what will it be like to have children with this person? What will it be like to grow old with him or her? Maybe his obsession with Super Mario Bros. is cute now, but will it be cute in ten years if he is lazy and doesn't want to work? Maybe you are able to excuse her road rage now, but will her anger find its way to you or your children in the future?

Our married friends are right: we need to realize what a big decision it is to marry someone and take practical steps toward making that decision with clear headed wisdom.

Let's remember to invite discernment on our dates and wisdom to the wedding.

Oh my gosh, I just saw my future. It involved me saying that phrase with a puppet on my hand on a Christian cable show called "Kate's Corner o' Dating Wisdom." Should I be scared, or should I get plastic surgery?

4.) Wait to get engaged until the removal of the projections happens.

Some of the best advice I have ever heard about

dating comes from my brilliant counselor. She says that every couple goes through what she calls the *removal of the projections*. According to her, when you start to date someone, you project the very best version of yourself toward him or her. (Think e-harmony profile here.) You also project your own version of the perfect person onto the one you are with. You look at that person as perfect when that person really isn't. When you are first in love, it's easy to overlook or ignore weaknesses.

But when the removal of the projections happens, the projections on both sides come down, and you see and are seen as you really are, weaknesses and all. When this happens, both parties often try to control the other because both are desperately wanting to keep the projection going and to believe that the other is perfect. Both parties also want to maintain the belief that they themselves are perfect, too. At that point, according to my counselor, there either comes a point of acceptance or a point of separation. Of course, this cycle can happen several times in the course of a relationship.

From my counselor's experience, it is much healthier to have the removal of the projections happen while a couple is dating rather than after the pair gets married. If it happens while dating, there is great security in knowing that your potential partner wants to be with you even if you are not perfect. Or, the removal of the projections can be a mirror that will help you break up if you realize that you aren't a good fit and that a marriage with this person would be extremely difficult.

If the removal of the projections happens after marriage, however, it can be really scary because you can feel trapped. Of course, if you are married you can choose to love the person regardless of what arises, but it makes sense to me that it would be a good goal to have enough time and experience to let at least the initial removal of the projections happen while dating.

5.) *Explore what it means to be in covenant, even before you are in one.*

This point closely relates to having the right expectations about marriage. This is not Hollywood, people; it is covenant. Covenant is hard work, and it is beautiful work.

Danny Silk provides a good definition of covenant as a "binding agreement that requires death."[37]

In Genesis 15, after God tells Abraham that his descendants would outnumber the stars, he seals this covenant by having Abraham sacrifice several animals. This was the first covenant that God made with Abraham, and it required death.

Throughout the Old Testament, we see a lot more covenant requiring a lot more death. God regularly commands an animal sacrifice to be made in the outer courts in order for the priest to go into the Holy of Holies and speak with him. And what was the name of the place that God dwelled? The Ark of the *Covenant*.

Most importantly, in the most stunning act of commitment in history, Jesus came to die so that our covenant with him would be sealed.

A definition of marriage that includes the word "death" is a lot harder to swallow than a definition that includes lots of roses, sex all the time, and the ability to use all of those two-for-one coupons we've saved for ten years. It is important for us to prepare for the beautiful difficulty that is waiting for us on the other side of covenant. When we say yes to our potential spouse, we are saying yes to serving and sacrificing in ways that we have never understood before.

My friend Brandon said to me the other day that there is a difference between contract and covenant. A contract, by definition, he said, involves an agreement that stands as long as each party lives up to their side of the bargain. Covenant, however, says, "You are family to me. Even if there are times when you don't live up to your part of the bargain, you are still my family."

Covenant is not just about receiving; it is about giving. Covenant is a lot like kissing. You can kiss someone because it feels nice to have his lips on yours (a fact that sounds really strange when you think about it), or you can kiss someone because you want to bless him with your affection. In one situation, you are kissing out of selfishness. In another, you are kissing for greater intimacy. Either way, you're getting kissed back.

If you are holding on to someone for reasons other than because you want to bring beautiful things to his or her life, you should examine your motivation. (I can relate to this because there have been times in my life when I stayed with a boyfriend not because we were a good match and because we would bless each other's lives, but because I really wanted to be married. This is not a good reason to stay together.)

Conversely, if you get the feeling your potential spouse is marrying you in order to feel valuable or because that person likes your 1976 El Camino, I beg you . . . run away fast!

But if you are in this thing to better each other's lives. Well, that can grow into something beautiful.

As a group of philosophers who went by the name DC Talk said many years ago, "Love is a Verb." Love is not just about feeling good; it's about a choice to commit.

6.) Realize that love is not only about taking a bullet for someone, but it is also about taking out the trash.

When I worked with InnerCHANGE, there was a great sign hanging over the kitchen sink that said, "Everyone wants to start a revolution, but nobody wants to do the dishes." (That sign guilted a lot of revolutionary, social-justice-hipster-Christians to buckle down and get that crusty cheese off of their bowl.)

This sign makes a good point: Big sacrifices are sometimes easier to make than small sacrifices. We all think that we would do something noble for someone we love, like throw our bodies over them while a double agent from Belarus tries to shoot them with a semi-automatic. The truth is, the double-agent-to-normal-citizen ratio is very low. Odds are we will never have to do anything like that.

However, if we have children, odds are we will have to wake up in the middle of the night to calm down a screaming baby about 835 times. I promise you, men, that if you get up and do that, you will be more of a hero to your sleep-deprived wife than you would be if you ran in front of a train to rescue her favorite Gucci bag. This is the point of this piece of advice from my married friends.

As we think about our future and present families, we'd do well to listen to this advice: If you want to love your family well, commit to doing thoughtful and uncomfortable things on a daily basis. Taking out the trash may not seem valiant, but when you do it to show respect and love to your family, it adds up to an important sacrifice.

The definition of heroic may be to take a bullet for someone, but the definition of integrity is to make small choices every day that bring honor to the people you love. That is something to remember whether we are married or not.

7.) Learn to communicate.

This nugget of advice is a big one for me. When I was growing up, the only time I can remember having a family meeting was when my parents told us they were getting a divorce. In my family, confrontation often meant harsh arguing. When there wasn't arguing, there was silence. In my mind, confrontation equalled trauma. No wonder I grew up terrified of communicating. No wonder I have to work through my feelings of being terrified of communicating now.

No problem, though. All I have to do is stuff my feelings and never talk about them, right? Well, if I want unhealthy relationships forever, I can stick with that plan. But I love people. I want to connect. And the only way that I can connect is to communicate.

After working through a lot of these issues the last few years, I have gotten much better at communicating. It has changed my life.

If you haven't looked at the very short chapter called "How to Communicate," read it again. Learning these four simple steps will help you walk the road toward communicating well.

I'll recap. First, *show up*. Showing up simply means to choose not to hide from conflict and to make space for communication to happen. Remember that the more you hide what is going on inside of you, the less alive you are. Second, *tell your truth*. In order to tell your truth, you have to take good inventory of what is going on inside you. Figure out what you are feeling and speak it out. Don't tell someone what you think that person wants to hear; tell the truth that is going on inside you. Third, *trust God*. And fourth, *let go of the outcome*. This means that you realize you can never control someone's response to what you say, and you can't control what happens after you say it. All you can control is what you say and how you respond.

Even though these steps are a good guideline for communicating well, there is so much more to learn about communication and lots of good resources to help us. I think it would be very wise of us to follow the advice of our married friends by committing to read books and listen to teachings on communication even before we are married.

If our goal is to love well, there is nothing more important than to work on being a good communicator.

8.) Make a commitment to learn your partner's code book.

In Dann Farrelly's teaching "Brave Communication," which is the best and most practical teaching on communication that I have ever heard, he talks about how every person has what he calls a "code book" that contains the person's perspective on life. Parents, classmates, teachers, past girlfriends or boyfriends, habits developed as children, and cultural expectations all contribute to this book. By the time a person is an adult, this book is as thick as a phone book and is very, very complicated. When two people's code books come together, those unique perspectives can be difficult to unite and may cause a lot of miscommunication.

Here is a good example of the clash of the code books: I had a boyfriend once who, every time we got off the phone said, "See ya." I hated it. I hated it when we first started dating, and I hated it even more after we were dating for a year.

Being a typical idealistic girl, I wanted him to end our conversations saying, "You are the most beautiful woman on earth. In fact, you are more like a goddess than a mere woman. Your absence is like a thread that weaves through the very fiber of my being. So for now, farewell, my love. I wait for the moment I see you again, for that is the moment I will come back to life."

Instead, I got "See ya."

I admit, some of my frustration with this salutation had to do with deeper issues that involved my wondering if he loved me or not. But there was also an element of the code book going on, too. I started noticing that every person in his family also ended conversations with the same nonchalance. Eventually, I realized that in my code book, "See ya" was a flippant thing said to an acquaintance, and it made me feel devalued. But in his code book, it was the equivalent of saying "goodnight" or "goodbye." Understanding his code book helped us relate to each other with more understanding and love.

So I think what Dann is getting at here is that we should be aware when something our partner does that frustrates us is truly an issue with sin and when it is simply an issue with his or her code book. An important part of being in a relationship is learning to love the other person enough to start reading through that person's code book and to be compassionate toward that person's perspective and journey.[38]

9.) Marriage is like driving.

When my friend Halen was about to get married, we all gave her marriage advice at her bachelorette party. As you can tell from this book, I am the queen of giving advice about things that I don't have much experience with. Romantic relationships, for example. But the advice that came out of my mouth that night made a lot of sense, and I'm going to pass it on to you. Therefore, this particular point of the chapter is not coming from a married person, but it is still worth listening to.

This is what I told her: Dating and marriage might seem pretty terrifying. It's all so risky! How could you possibly foresee and prepare for the problems you might have? Maybe it would be helpful to think about relationships the same way you think about driving. What if I was so scared of driving that I never left home? What if I said, "I can't do this whole traveling thing! A blue-haired lady might come out of nowhere and try to get in my lane! A biker might ride dangerously close to me! I might get both of my hands tied up while I'm taking my coat off! That's it. I'm staying home."

"It *is* risky to drive," I told Halen. "But there is something that, as drivers, we all understand: we can't possibly foresee the problems that will come before we are actually on the road. We have to get in the car and take the problems as we go, overcoming them one by one. We see a yellow light, and we slow down. We see a biker, and we get out of the way. We see a blue-haired lady, and we pass her so that we do not have endure 35 mph commutes."

What I'm saying is, yes, it could save us getting into a bad accident to review the rules of driving on a regular basis. Yes, it would be wise to look at a map if we don't know where we are going. But worrying about problems you cannot foresee will stop you from ever taking any risks. And a life without risks is no life at all.

When you worry, you fear something that has not happened yet. Odds are, it won't happen. What a horrible way to spend your time. Mark Twain supposedly said, "I've had thousands of problems in my life, most of which never actually happened."

You can only eat an elephant one bite at a time. Your job is not to avoid risk and stay home. Your job is to get in the car and do the next right thing. Sometimes the next right thing is to overcome fear and commit to someone. And even after that, all you have to do is the next right thing.

Doesn't that make all of this dating and marrying stuff a little less scary? It does for me.

10.) *Remember, there are never perfect matches, but there are good matches.*

According to my married friends, it is impossible to find the perfect person to be with. There are no perfect people. Every person on earth is going to have some traits you like and some traits you don't like.

There is a popular concept out there that I'm sure you are familiar with, the idea of "the one." This idea says that there is one and only one person who is your soul mate. There is no one else out there that is right for you, so you better look hard for the one. Most married people I talked to no longer believe in this concept. In fact, divorced friends of mine have told me they think that believing in "the one" can hurt marriages. According to them, when a marriage gets difficult it is easy to think, *Oh no! Maybe this is not the one! Maybe I should leave this person so I can find the one!*

I personally believe that it is less helpful to ask yourself if a potential mate is the one and more helpful to ask if that person is a good match or a bad match.

Let me give you an example in my own life of a bad match. I was with a man for a long time who was very different than me. He was logical and analytical. We would sort through issues for hours at a time. We tried really hard to come to agreements with each other. He loved to discuss things. Now, I like discussing things, but I also really like to have fun. I felt like I was losing my sense of humor, and he didn't feel like he could be as analytical as he wanted to be.

After a while, it was clear that our issues were not merely code book issues. We were just not a good match for each other. I beat myself up, thinking I had done something wrong or that I had been someone wrong. But the truth was, we would probably have had a really hard time if we had gotten married, even if we really loved each other.

It was not our fault. We were just not a good match. Some people's personalities simply go together better. There is no rhyme or reason to this. Chemistry is a real thing, and so is compatibility.

How can you tell if the person you are dating is a bad match for you? First, you need to ask yourself if you can handle the hard things times ten. If you get married, you will probably have to deal with them times ten. You also need to weigh that person's good qualities against the bad, deciding if the good is worth the bad. These are all things you can only learn with good information as you date someone.

Again, take inventory to decide if you are jumping to the conclusion that you are not a good match just because you are scared to commit. If you have given it time and have gotten good information about one another and it still feels like trying to hammer a round peg into a square hole, however, do not beat yourself up. It may simply be that you are just not compatible.

11.) *Go on a road trip to Coney Island.*

I am a traveller. I refuse to believe that I will never do anything adventurous again after I have a family. I have seen people travel with families. In fact, my dear friend's baby has been to more countries than I have, and he's only one year old. He has been to ten countries and twenty states! Getting married does not have to mean that all things fun in life cease to exist. I might have to make a conscious decision to get out the door with my family and go camping rather than to obsess over the stain that won't come out of the kitchen floor, but I can do it.

Despite this, married people have suggested that I come to grips with the fact that my life will be drastically different if I get married and have children.

I know, I know. We singles hate it when marrieds tell us that we should do everything we can while we are single because we have loads of extra time. We often think that we've had enough adventures and just want to have babies.

We also wonder why our married friends say stuff like that. I don't feel like I have lots of time! But I guess, really, I do have more time than most of my married friends because I can usually make boundaries and say no to things in order to have more time. They often can't. When little Tommy is wiping his diaper on the wall, for example. You really can't say no to that. You have to deal with it.

I will let you in on a little secret. I expect that our married friends tell us that we should have lots of adventures before we are married because they really, honestly mean it. They miss having more freedom.

Covenant by the very nature of the word is constraining. It implies having new, stricter boundaries. In marriage you take the other person's life, preferences, schedule, and a million other things and make them your own. Those things, compiled with having the responsibility of bringing several small human beings into the place we call planet Earth and helping them comprehend the meaning of life, along with feeding them strained carrots, can really be a time suck. That is not just something our married friends say to amuse us or make us mad. It is the truth.

Maybe we should get over ourselves, go to Coney Island with our roommates, and thoroughly enjoy ourselves.

12.) Try to be a true helpmate for your partner.

I want to end with this point because it so beautifully sums up what a good relationship should look like.

The Hebrew word "helpmate" comes from two words in Hebrew, "ezar" (which means "power, strength") and "kenegdo" (which means, "who stands opposite and looks in the face").[39]

We often think that the word "helpmate" denotes that one person is under the other. The true essence of the word, however, is that there are two whole people—equals—who are strong for themselves and strong for the other. They stand opposite of each other, and, in doing so, they look each other in the face. Their being opposite of each other is not a bad thing; it gives them strength. Because they are opposite, they are able to look behind their beloved to see what their beloved cannot see and protect them from it. The more these two communicate with each other, the more they are able to learn from the perspective of the one that stands opposite of them.

This beautifully depicts what we should strive for in any relationship. We are to work toward wholeness, toward being strong in ourselves so that we can be strong for each other. We are to be confident in our stance, standing opposite but learning to communicate so that our differences add to the other person's life. We are to look at the person in the face, an act that depicts both vulnerability and intimacy. We are to dance together, a dance in which our opposite natures bring beauty rather than strife.

This is some of the wonderful advice that I have received from my married friends, and I intend to learn from it whether I get married or not.

Chapter Eleven

Throw Away Your List
(Or Just Rewrite It)

Ashley was shipwrecked on the Isle of Singleness. She was stranded there for a long time and was very lonely. She prayed, saying, "God, please send a perfect man to get me off of this island."

Soon, a man in a speedboat came along. He was very kind and dedicated. But he was listening to Celine Dion on the radio.

He said, "Ashley, I have come a very long way to take you off of this island."

She told him, "Thanks for the offer, but God is going to send me the perfect man. And the perfect man cannot be listening to bad diva music."

Soon, another man came in a rowboat. He was great with children and had a wonderful sense of humor. But he was balding a little bit. He said, "My darling Ashley. I have rowed many hundreds of miles to rescue you off of this island."

She replied, "I appreciate what you have done, but God is going to send me the perfect man to get me off of this island. He has to have hair in all of the right places. Namely a lot on his head, and none on his back. Now why don't you just take your little bald head and row right back to the mainland."

Finally, a man came swimming to the shore. He had a huge heart and incredible faith. Breathless, he threw his arms around her and said, "Ashley, you are the woman of my dreams. I swam five hundred miles, and then I swam five hundred more just to be the man to swim a thousand miles and fall down at your door. I also strapped a romantic picnic dinner, your hairdryer, and your favorite chick flicks on my back."

Ashley replied, "What, no flowers?"

Ashley stayed on the island many years. Finally she shook her fist at the sky: "God, why haven't you sent me the perfect man to get me off of this island?"

He said, "I sent you a potential husband in a speedboat, a potential husband in a rowboat, and a potential husband who swam a thousand miles to fall down at your door."

"But God," Ashley replied, "none of those men fit everything on my list!"

God said, "If you ever want to get off of this island, you're going to have to write a new list."*

---

* This is a little story I wrote that is based on a joke I've heard in church a few times. In the joke, a man is hanging on a branch, about to fall off a cliff into the ocean. He prays to God for help. He is subsequently sent different rescue missions, including two different boats and a helicopter. Each time he refuses the help, saying "God is going to save me." When he finally dies, he asks God why he wasn't given any help, and God says "I sent you two boats and a helicopter! What more did you want?!" I thought this tied in nicely with what we are discussing in this chapter. Sometimes, we don't see God's provision even when it is right in front of us because it looks different than we expected it to look.

I have a journal for my husband that I started when I was twenty-one. I poured my heart out to this journal. What was in my heart at the time was a considerable amount of romantic nonsense.

I haven't told many people this, but toward the beginning of this journal, I wrote a song for my future husband. It's called, *Made as One*. I wrote the first verse and the chorus, but I never wrote the second verse. On purpose. You know why? My plan was to write the second verse on the day my future husband asked me to marry him. I mean, how romantic is that? How much would my husband swoon when I sang it at our wedding? To hear this beautiful song that had been written for him over time, ending with the crescendo of our perfect union?

I secretly had a good idea of what the lines of that second verse would be, even though I was waiting to write them.

They would go something like this:

> *It's been two years since I wrote those words*
> *You asked me to marry you tonight.*
> *I never knew my heart could feel like this*
> *I never knew our love could take such flight.*

Or some such cheese.

But now that song will have to be different than I expected. And it would be less catchy:

> *It's been twelve years since I wrote those words*
> *Kind of funny we're middle aged*
> *If we had waited much longer dear,*
> *You'd have to buy me some BENGAY®.*

A lot of popular music genres have come and gone since I started the song, so now it sounds quite dated. In fact, now that I think about it, it sounds almost exactly like a bad Journey song.

I am not singing that thing at my wedding. No way.

And, of course, there is more than just the song in my journal. Tucked carefully away between the pages of that journal is . . . the list.

All you females out there, and probably a lot of the males, you know exactly what I'm talking about when I say that. You know what the list is because you have your own list that, most likely, is not that different from mine.

The list is a series of characteristics that I want in my future spouse.

Here is a composite of a few items on my list and on the lists of some friends I interviewed:

1.) He must be taller than me.

2.) He must be strong.

3.) He must have black hair and blue eyes.

4.) He must have nice nails.

5.) He must look good in a suit.

6.) He must not watch a lot of football.

7.) He has to love dogs.

8.) He has to have a college education.

9.) He has to be an avid reader.

10.) He has to make a lot of money.

11.) He must be willing to massage my feet.

12.) He can never use the term "lol" in his texts.

13.) He must not have hair on his chest.

14.) He must not have any hair in his ears or nose or on his back. Ever.

15.) He must have hair on his head.

16.) He must be a pro-skiing, TV-avoiding, muscle-flexing, chore-doing, model-looking, eternal giver of romance and love and passion.

17.) He can't snore.

18.) Lastly, and under no circumstances, will I ever ever be intimate with someone who wears novelty socks.

Sound familiar?

Years ago a good friend of mine and I had some sparks flying around us for a while. One day, however, while eating lunch together, he started chewing with his mouth open a little bit. A man who chews with his mouth open was definitely not on my list. To make matters worse, he also had a pretty serious pimple on his face that day. Also not on my list.

So, I ended up going for another guy who was much more suave than the first one. The second guy broke my heart after we dated for nine months. The pimple guy who chewed with his mouth open moved away and is now married with a few kids. He is an incredible dad, an incredible husband, and loves the Lord very much.

I have quite a few things that I would tell the younger version of myself, and this would be one of them: marrying someone who has perfect table manners is not really going to matter in forty years. What is going to matter is that my partner is kind and has integrity and that we love being with each other.

I know now that habits can change. I can tell my partner that I'd feel loved if he tried not to show me the gumbo in his mouth. Table manners may be able to be tamed in just a few conversations. But turning a mean guy into a nice guy?

A lifetime. Which one do I want on my list?

When we are young, we think there will always be potential suitors and that we need to wait for the perfect one. But at my age, we realize that dating should not be about finding someone perfect. It should be about finding a good match.

I had a forty-something male friend write me the other day about this very topic. This is what he wrote:

> Women at church seem to have a list that personifies their perfect man. These ladies won't take a risk on a guy who is not good-looking, who is balding, who can't play guitar, can't dance, or who has a gap in his teeth. All because of their list.

He went on to talk about how he has gone on a few dates with women who weren't believers. These women were much more open to actually seeing his heart, mostly because they didn't have their God-has-the-perfect-man-for-me glasses on. He didn't commit to these women, however, because he knew he couldn't compromise his faith. But he reflected in his letter to me, he wished that he could find a woman with a strong faith who was also willing to see past his bald spot and into his heart. He concluded the letter saying, "Women want to be pursued, but not by a man who isn't handsome enough for them."

It is a little scary writing a book because I know that advice I give might potentially change the course of someone's life. I don't want people to say, "Hey, that *Getting Naked Later* girl said I shouldn't be too picky or else I'll be thirty-something and alone. So I'd better marry my loser boyfriend as soon as possible." Therefore, I'm going to make myself very clear. When I say that you shouldn't be too picky, I am not saying that you should settle. It is incredibly dangerous to settle. I myself could have married quite a few men who would not have been good for me. Those breakups were not about me being too picky; they were about me being smart. Even worse than marrying a man who is not a good fit is marrying someone who is toxic. Settling for a spouse who is unkind or severely addicted can be the most devastating decision of your life.

Let's learn not to be picky when it comes to the shallow things and to be very picky when it comes to the important things. That is the balance.

This point is well-illustrated in this real-life letter sent to an advice columnist:

Dear Amy,

I've been dating a man on and off for at least fifteen years. He let me know on the first date that he's a "Confirmed Bachelor." I'm single, too. Sometimes I don't hear from him for more than a year. And then he'll call to go out. Do you think I should always go out with him when he calls? I don't want to seem desperate. Also, do you think I should call him when I don't hear from him? I don't want him to think I'm a chaser. I like him very much and I find him very interesting to talk to. He's also very smart and I like a smart man . . . So far, we've had a very platonic relationship.[40]

You don't want to seem desperate? Sister, you've been waiting for this man for years. I've got news for you: You *are* desperate. He's interesting to talk to? OK, you can check that off of your list. He's smart? Fine, you can check that off, too. But those two attributes are not enough on which build a relationship. You need to add a few things to your list like, he's emotionally available and he calls weekly instead of annually and he doesn't tell me on the first date that he will never be committed to me.

Why do we do this? Why do we skip over people who could be good for us just because we don't have "that gut feeling" from the first few dates? Why are we drawn to people who we know are not good for us and stay with them? I think that in the first wakes of love, we convince ourselves that the latter group fits our list more than the first group. We convince ourselves that there is no one else for us.

When we're in love, it is hard to be practical. But we must force ourselves to be practical when making a decision that is this important.

As I said in the last chapter, there is true wisdom in looking for the fruit of something when it is still a seed. If you see deep-seated character issues—such as unkindness—that could be really difficult down the road, get out. I am serious. Out.

If fifteen of your dear friends tell you that they feel like your current relationship will really turn out to be a bad thing—that this guy you are dating is actually a jerk—they probably can see something that you don't in your tunnel-of-love vision. Get out. I am serious. Out.

Where is the balance? What is the happy medium

between having totally unrealistic expectations for anyone you date and marrying someone who will most likely be really hard to live with, who might even be a nightmare to live with?

In my opinion, one of the best solutions is to rewrite your list. Pare it down to four or five nonnegotiables.

Here are the nonnegotiables that I have chosen for my own spouse, if I do decide to get married.

1.) He must have a deep love for God and for people.

2.) He must be kind.

3.) We need to enjoy being with each other. Evidence of this would be laughing together, having good conversations, and dealing with conflict well.

4.) He needs to see the world as a place to explore and as a place to bring hope. I want his vision to be to bring love to the community around us, whether that be in small ways or big ways. I honestly could care less if we make a lot of money. That is not a priority for me. My priority is that we make the world a better place together.

I can't think of much else that matters other than the qualities on my new short list. Balding? He can shave his head—that can be sexy. Chewing with his mouth open? We can talk about that. Celine Dion? He can listen to her on his earphones all his heart desires. Snoring? I can wear earplugs. If he has the qualities that are on my new list, I will go on some dates with him. I will give him a chance.

I know that writing a new list is not a fool-proof plan for finding a quality spouse. I realize that many of you out there married someone who you thought was a really good choice but turned out not to be. I understand that we can't see the future. But we can try our best to look for the fruit of something when it is still a seed.

Give your seed time to grow. That way you can consciously make a commitment using both your heart and your head.

A little eight-year-old girl was asked what she thought love was. She cocked her head and thought for a little bit. Then she replied, "When my grandmother got arthritis, she couldn't bend over to paint her toenails anymore. So my grandfather does it for her all the time, even when his hands got arthritis. That's what love is."[41]

Look for someone who will love you like this little girl's grandpa loved his wife. Look for a seed that will end in this kind of fruit. Don't just look for a spouse that you are lightening-flash attracted to. Don't just look for someone who says all the perfect things at the perfect time and gives you dozens of roses. Don't just look for someone who fits everything on your ridiculously long, shallow list. Look for someone who will paint your toenails when you're old even though he has arthritis.

Because that's what love is.

How to Date

1.) Go out, give the person a chance.

2.) Make clear boundaries. Communicate well.

3.) Get good information day by day.

4.) When you get enough information to know if it's a good match or not, decide whether to get married or to break up.

Chapter Twelve

'90s Dating Gone Bad

One of the most popular Christian dating books of all time is called *I Kissed Dating Goodbye*. It was written in 1997 by a twenty-one-year-old man named Joshua Harris. It discussed the many reasons why he thought dating was a bad, even an ungodly, idea.

The cover of the book had a picture of a man with a mysterious hat over his eyes and a very, very nice jawline. I really wanted to date him. On the back of the book was a snapshot of the very handsome young author looking wistfully into the camera with his innocent brown eyes. Definitely wanted to date him, too. If the Christian book publisher really wanted me to kiss dating goodbye, it would have been wise for them to put uglier guys on the cover.

The book turned into a Christian phenomenon that turned into a bunch of rules that turned into a tsunami from whose wake the Christian dating pool is still recovering. I do want to add here that I believe this book can be helpful for teenagers who are trying to navigate dating, but for adults it just doesn't make very much sense.

Even though the rules that were established in the era of Harris' book were much more popular fifteen years ago, their weirdness still affects us. Without knowing it, we have become the Frankenstein children of bad '90s dating. Being aware of these rules will help us understand why some of us have green skin and bolts coming out of our necks when we date.

Let's look at some of rules of this "no dating tolerance" era and learn from them so we can date better now.

1.) God needs to tell us, often through signs, who we are going to marry.

About ten years ago, my boyfriend Ken and I were contemplating marriage. I was as a scared as a pregnant porcupine.

Back then, I would pray for signs all the time: "God, if you really want me to marry him, please have someone stand on their head in the middle of this convenience store." Stuff like that.

I fasted several times for the relationship, begging for signs from God. I did one especially long fast during which I started out with water only. Soon, I was throwing cherry pie into the blender. I was on the verge of trying a steak smoothie when I finally got my answer in the middle of the night. I had a dream that I opened my Bible to IV Chronicles.

That was the whole dream.

I woke up the next day, and, being the astute Christian scholar that I am, I realized that there is, in fact, no IV Chronicles. So I looked up I Chronicles 4 instead.

These were the shocking words that I read that day:

> The sons of Judah: Pharez, Hezron, and Carmi, and Hur, and Shobal [. . .]These are the families of the Zorathites (I Chronicles 4:1-2, KJV).

Bingo. That was it. I was supposed to marry him.

OK, that's not really what happened. I was more like, "What the heck is this? Come on, God. I wanted a sign and I got a bunch of begets!"

Almost as a joke, I said, "God, if I'm supposed to marry Ken, put a version of his name in here."

I turned the page and there it was, clear as day.

> "These are the men of Rechah. And the sons of *Kenaz* . . ." (I Chronicles 4:12b-13a, KJV).

Kenaz certainly sounded like the Hebrew version of Ken to me. I had my answer.

What happened next? I will give you one hint: I am still single and it is ten years later.

Another serious boyfriend and I—let's call him Jordan—were praying about whether or not we should get married. During the course of our relationship, he had really struggled with whether he loved me or not. We had separated into different cities for a season—you know, the whole we're-taking-a-break-to-pray deal that actually means we're freaking out. We had met together to reevaluate, and he said that he wanted to move to my town and pursue our relationship one more time. I was worried that he would still struggle with whether he loved me or not, and so I was very hesitant for him to move.

Jordan and I decided to pray about it for a few weeks. In the meantime, I looked for signs like a near-sighted truck driver.

I got the sign I was looking for when I went to visit my mom and we played a game of Boggle together. If you haven't seen Boggle before, it has a covered tray of sixteen cubic dice with letters on them. You shake the dice, and they fall into place on the grid of the tray. Players compete to find short words.

My mom and I played one round in which, clear as day, she found the words "Jordan is in love" on the little squares. I mean, out of millions of combinations of letters, those were the ones that happened to be rolled. I have the picture to prove it. What are the odds of that?

I had my sign, and my mom had twenty more Boggle points.

Despite the sign, Jordan and I broke up three weeks later.

A year after we broke up, I showed some friends a picture of the Boggle game.

They looked at the picture carefully.

"Oh yeah! There's 'Jordan,' see it? And there's 'is' and 'in' and 'love.' That is crazy, Kate!"

They passed the Boggle picture on to my friend Aaron, who noticed something important: "Kate, there is another word in here that you missed. The word 'not.'"

I looked at the picture, and, sure enough, there it was—a very important word that I had missed for an entire year: n-o-t.

Depending on how astute I was at the game of Boggle, I could have read the sentence "Jordan is in love" or "Jordan is *not* in love." Wow. Can you spell D-A-N-G-E-R-O-U-S?

This story clearly illustrates the fact that we often look for signs that tell us what we want to see. When it comes to something as important as marriage, this is a risky way to make decisions. The truth is, a sign might be good information, but it is not even close to all the information you need to assess whether or not a person is a wise choice for a future mate.

The moral of the story? Don't let a Boggle game tell your future.

Not only is asking for signs to make decisions dangerous, it can also be immature.

I Corinthians 13:11 says, "When I was a child, I talked like a child, I thought like a child, I reasoned like a child. When I became a man, I put childish ways behind me" (NIV). You may tell a little child "don't touch that" when that child is about to stick a finger in a light socket, but when that child becomes an adult, you know that adult is wise enough not to touch the light socket. In the same way, when we become spiritually mature enough to self-govern, it is time to move on to a new model for dating—one that goes beyond signs and becomes suitable for thinking adults. One in which we make decisions *with* God instead of having him make decisions *for* us.

2.) Dating isn't biblical.

It is true that dating isn't biblical. It's not in the Bible. So maybe we should try a marriage philosophy that is in the Bible: polygamy. Abraham had one wife and one concubine. David had lots more. Solomon was the wisest man on earth, and he pretty much had an entire motel full of them. That's in the Bible, so it must be biblical. Taking up this biblical marriage practice would solve a lot of problems. We all know that there are probably about ten Christian women for every Christian man. If we just started practicing this tradition, voila! Problem solved!

Of course, I am exaggerating. We understand that polygamy is not a good idea. We understand that the practice was a part of Hebrew and surrounding cultures (mostly in the upper class) but that it was never necessarily God's best. Just because it is in the Bible does not mean that it is right. And conversely, just because it is not in the Bible does not mean that it is wrong.

American culture is very different than the culture of the Bible. When my dad wants to buy some land, he doesn't offer my hand in marriage along with twenty camels and a flock of sheep. Marriage is no longer a business proposition like it used to be. It is a search for a life companion.

Women are now able to make enough money to support themselves, and thus, they are not required to have a husband in order to survive. (Indeed, throughout history there were few alternatives for livelihood besides marriage and prostitution.) Women's rights have been one of the major factors that have brought us from a culture of arranged marriages to a culture in which people date to find a mate. Therefore, dating is not necessarily a bad institution, but rather it is an institution that has progressed as marriage has changed. An institution that now allows for a woman's choice rather than a woman's obedience.

Those who favor courtship over dating may argue that the way the western world dates now ends in a fifty percent divorce rate. I would absolutely agree with them. We live in a culture that is so set on experiencing pleasure that people often stomp on anyone they love to get it. Many people sleep around as if sex were as much of a commitment as buying a cup of coffee in the morning. Some people seem to try spouses on, only to throw them out as if they were jeans that have gone out of style. There is little or no value for covenant in American popular culture, and the sacred institution of marriage is often joked about. I know that this is not the best way. Jesus weeps when relationships are this broken, and so do I.

At the same time, I don't want to go back to a time in which I am seen as a commodity—a time in which I have no say in a decision as important as marriage. Yes, I do agree that dating is an institution that has been abused. But I don't believe that because there are people around me abusing it or the media is abusing it that I have to abuse it.

Instead of seeing dating as unhealthy because it is not in the Bible or because people around us have abused it, perhaps we can use it as an effective tool in choosing a good partner. Perhaps we can have good boundaries in dating. Perhaps we can learn a lot about ourselves and about what match would make sense for us. Perhaps we can make wise, educated decisions because we have spent good time with different people and, ultimately, with the person we commit ourselves to. Dating can be very useful in our journeys of marrying well, if we use it the right way.

3.) You shouldn't date; you should court.

My friend Neal told me the other day that one of his coworkers who is "unchurched" read my blog (thesexyceli-bate.com) via a link on Neal's Facebook page. I perked up my ears, expecting Neal to tell me that my blog changed his friend's life. Not quite. In fact, what the coworker said was something like, "Neal, that's some weird crap on that blog."

I think it's time that we corporately admit that when it comes to dating, we Christians have all believed some weird crap. One of the weirdest things we have believed was this rule: since dating isn't biblical, you should court in order to pick your mate.

Let me tell you a story in order to illustrate how peculiar and sometimes damaging courting is. I was with my first serious boyfriend in college, and we were in the throes of first love. We often hung out with two other couples, the girls of which were my best friends. One of the couples was on the verge of getting engaged.

One weekend, our boyfriends went together to a men's retreat. The speaker announced that dating wasn't biblical, and our passionate, naïve men decided that they should keep each other accountable to breaking up with us that very day.

One dumped woman is bad. But three simultaneously-dumped women? That, my friends, is a nightmare.

Needless to say, the three of us girls gathered together after that horrible night and became a heaping pile of feminine despair. Our now ex-boyfriends were shocked that we reacted with so much emotion. I think they were expecting us to say, "Thank you for showing what godly men you are by breaking up with us. That was so noble of you!"

Instead, we wanted to slash their tires.

The three men got together and discussed the issue again. They came back to us and said that they didn't have to break up with us if they could court us instead of date us. We were so relieved. There was only one problem: none of us knew what courting was. Within a few weeks, our courting life looked pretty much exactly like our dating life, except it was called something different.

Recently I remembered this incident and wanted to better understand the history of courting. I found out some surprising things. The word "courting" is not in the Bible, just like the word "dating" is not in the Bible. Almost all marriages were arranged in biblical times. I then realized that the main model for the Christian concept of courting looks more like Amish culture than biblical culture. Contrary to what you might think, though, the Amish version of courting seems to be more healthy and even more modern than does the weird Christian version.

Amish young people get together most Sundays after church for socials. Aha, you say! Group dating! Just like Joshua Harris told us to date! But that is not the end of the story. If two people are interested in getting to know each other, they can go in a courting buggy, which is an open horse-drawn carriage. They ride in the buggy and talk; they might hold hands. According to a National Geographic documentary called "Amish at the Altar," going on a buggy ride does not mean that the pair will marry. Their system is much more casual than that. During their courting years, they will usually go on buggy rides with several different people. In fact, the parents don't often know who their kids are going on buggy rides with until they get serious about one of their options. Buggy rides are simply a way to get to know someone.[42]

I think the Amish way of courting makes more sense than the courting that I was taught. Our strict '90s Christian dating style mandated that a man and woman should not often be alone and that they shouldn't spend intentional time with each other unless they were pretty sure they were going to get married. In contrast, there doesn't seem to be a lot of pressure if you buggy with someone. You are just getting to know them. You are just gathering some information about whether the person you are riding in the buggy with would be a good match. There are strong boundaries, but you also have lots of alone time with that person to focus on conversing and getting good information about that person.

(I will mention here that according to the same *National Geographic* documentary, the rare Amish community does accept the practice of bundling or "bed courting," which involves a courting couple sleeping in the same bed as long as both people are clothed and the woman has the sheets to herself. I'm not sure if this is a good rule for me. My inner dragon might come out in that situation. And my inner dragon is not Amish.)

One of my blog readers the other day commented that

we should start a revolution that is more realistic than courting but more committed than dating. I like her idea of balance. As I have mentioned previously, balance is a good rule of thumb for almost everything in life.

But then I pictured my book becoming a phenomenon like *I Kissed Dating Goodbye,* where people started a revolution to do something new—something right in the middle of dating and courting, like my reader suggested.

Maybe they would call it dorting! Or catering! Oh wait, that doesn't work. How about buggying! That's it! Buggying!

Then people would say, "Hey, I really don't want to date you, and I don't really want to court you, either. I want to be right in the middle. I want to buggy you. We could cruise around in my convertible with the top down so people can see us—that way we are in a semi-public place but still alone. What do you think?"

Then I realized that I didn't want that to happen, either. You know why?

Because that's some weird crap, y'all.

Let's just be adults and date well. How does that sound?

4.) *You should never be alone with a person of the opposite sex because you don't want to end up having premarital sex.*

You may have noticed that for a book with the word "naked" in it and for a girl whose blog name involves the word "sexy," there is very little in this book about sex. At first I felt like I should have at least one chapter dedicated to that subject. But then I realized that I am actually really private when it comes to those things. In fact, I wrote a sentence with the word "virgin" in it earlier and I ended up erasing it. I don't even know you people! Why am I telling you the status of my sexuality?

To be perfectly honest, I don't know a lot about sex. I don't know enough to write a whole chapter on the subject, let alone a whole book. (Which, I guess, is what you might have been expecting when you picked up this book. Sorry if I disappointed you.)

But I do think I can muster up a few paragraphs. Here goes . . .

I have lived my life with the philosophy that sex is something incredibly sacred. So sacred, in fact, that I have chosen to be that imitate only with someone inside the boundaries of a life-long covenant. I have made that choice not simply because it is what my Christian culture expects me to do; I have chosen it because I know having sex with a man (or several men) who are not in covenant with me would be very, very hard on my heart. I also know that having sex could put me in very difficult situations that I may not be prepared for. I want to be wise when it comes to what I do with my body. It's the only body I have, after all.

I have also chosen abstinence because covenant is serious to God, and there is nothing else on earth that seals a covenant in the same way that sex does. This is why it is especially devastating that our modern society treats sex so casually. Many people have taken something incredibly mysterious and sacred and have turned it into something common. That is infinitely sad to me, and it is infinitely sad to the God who created that sacred union. I have chosen to see sex as sacred because my God sees it as sacred. If that means waiting, I will wait.

Yes, there are days when abstinence is a difficult choice.

There are days when society makes me feel like I am not a whole person because I haven't had sex. There are days in springtime when I wonder if every adult animal in the world is having sex except me. There are days when a man touches my arm for just a second, and I realize how good it feels to have someone's skin on mine. And then I remember how seldom touch is a part of my life, and I realize how much I ache to have someone hold me.

Despite these things, for the most part, I have found abstinence to be a good choice for me. I think that waiting for marriage is a really good way to live, and I can back that up with my own choices.

After saying all that, I have to add that the '90s dating-gone-bad rules were very odd when it came to sex. The rules said that we should always group date or date in public. How are we ever supposed to get to know someone that way? Will we go to such lengths to avoid having sex that we march our innocent little butts down the aisle toward a person we barely know? Sex before marriage can be destructive, but so can marrying a person whose middle name you don't know until you are on your honeymoon.

As always, there needs to be balance. Balance between understanding the sacredness of sex and understanding the sacredness of knowing someone very well when you tie yourself to that person for life.

Here are two things that I think will help us in the quest for good physical boundaries when we date.

The first is to "know thyself."

These are Plato's words, and they are full of wisdom. Try to understand what is going on inside you when it comes to sex. Figure out what you can handle.

In my case, I know that I can make a boundary with someone I am dating and stick with it. I can kiss and have a lot of fun and intimacy, and I can back off and communicate when I think we might cross the boundaries we have set. Kissing the few men I have kissed has actually been healing for me. I have gone through certain things in my past that made me apprehensive of any kind of intimacy, but over the years I have dated trustworthy, kind men who respected the boundaries we set together, and God has brought a lot of healing through that, even though I didn't marry any of those men. I now really enjoy intimacy instead of being scared of it.

On the other hand, there may be some who cannot handle very much physical intimacy. Some folks want to make a sprint around the bases if their partner wears the right pair of earrings. Be honest with yourself. Communicate well with the person you are dating. Make boundaries together that you know you can follow.

The second thing that will help us in our quest for good physical boundaries is to foster a culture that does not succumb to the lie that we are slaves to sin.

Now, I don't want to downplay a subject that has been a life-long struggle for some people. I don't really understand what it's like to be someone who has been tortured by sex addictions or pornography. (Let me say that I applaud you for being brave and fighting for freedom from this.) I know that sex before marriage is tempting. I know that we need good boundaries. But I believe that one of the best ways to deal with this issue is to stop seeing ourselves as weak. We've got to stop telling ourselves that if we are left to our own devices we will have no choice but to lose ourselves to passion. We've got to stop acting like sexual desire is a force that takes over us and like we have no choice but to kneel as its slave.

If we see ourselves as people who have no control over ourselves, then we will be people who have no control over ourselves. We should start seeing ourselves for what we are: people who the Lord has made strong. People who have self-control and who do not need chastity belts in order to be in the same room with someone of the opposite sex. The more we see ourselves as weak, the weaker we will be. We must remember the truth: temptation does not have control over us. We have control over temptation.

I know it is unwise to sleep in the same bed, to be alone all the time, to go off for the weekend to some romantic place and think we won't be tempted. We don't want to set ourselves up to cross our boundaries, and there is something special about saving those activities for covenant. However, let's see ourselves as people who can have adult dating relationships that allow us to get to know each other very, very well before we get married without having to tear each other's clothes off before the wedding night.

Self-governing is always the kind of government that works the best, and this is very true when it comes to sex.

5.) *You should know whether you will get married or not within the first few dates.*

This is the rule that has seeped into our dating landscape more than any other. Men have an especially large amount of pressure on them in this regard when it comes to dating. If a man finally gets the nerve to ask out someone he likes, it's likely that, as a result of this silly rule, the bridesmaids dresses and china patterns are picked out after the first cup of coffee. Christian men often find themselves in a quandary thinking, *I want to get to know this girl, but if I ask her out, I need to be pretty sure that I'm serious about her. But how do I know if I am serious about her if I don't spend quality time with her?* It is a catch-22.

I would be scared too. See what a bunch of rules does to us?

The pressure from this rule is exacerbated by the "I just knew" phenomenon. We have all heard stories like, "I saw him across the fellowship hall as he was eating his doughnut. We started discussing predestination, and I knew then and there that *I* was *his* predestination. We were married three months later." Sure, this not-so-imaginary couple knew what they wanted right away and got it. But I wonder if those are also the kind of decisive people who see an outfit they like in the department store window, try it on, and immediately buy it. That decisiveness could be the way they make all their decisions. I, on the other hand, look at an outfit in several different mirrors for half an hour before I decide if I want it, and after I buy it, I still save my receipt for six months just in case I change my mind. I seem to date the same way.

The point is, we all have different decision-making methods, and we will probably use those when we date. For every "I just knew" story, there is a "I didn't think I liked him at all until I got to know him" story. If we give up right away because we want someone else's story, we might miss out on the really beautiful relationship that is uniquely meant for us.

Clearly, the combined formula of the "you shouldn't date

unless you know" rule and the "you should know right away" rule puts enormous pressure on the first stages of dating, a time that I think should start out as casual and fun.

In my opinion, it is far too dangerous to rush things when you are making a decision this important. When we date we should take the time to know someone day-to-day, getting good information until there is enough to make a wise choice.

I have heard over and over again in my interviews with married people that putting pressure on oneself to "know" after the first few dates can be very dangerous because it could mean rushing to get married too soon. I have tried to put that advice into practice by using a little tool I call the "holiday effect." I ask myself if there is enough enjoyment and beauty and mutual sharpening in this relationship that I would want to keep pursuing it to the next holiday. If the answer is yes, I invest wholeheartedly in the relationship day-by-day until the next holiday, and then I check what is going on with us as a couple and what is going on inside of me. I ask myself if we are a good match, if I am having fun, if the person I'm dating has integrity, and if I am feeling hesitant because we are not a good match or because I am scared of commitment. After I ask those questions, I keep doing the next best thing. Someday I will get enough information to know whether a future with this person is a good idea or not. Thinking this way helps keep myself in check if I find myself thinking about marriage too soon.

Marriage is serious business. A decision this important deserves respect and time. Getting good information is very important. I believe that the clearest way God can speak to us, rather than through signs similar to those we talked about earlier, is through us answering practical questions over time. How does my boyfriend treat his mother? How does my girlfriend handle stress? Am I terrified of committing? Why is that? Is my boyfriend kind to people even in difficult circumstances? Does my girlfriend make God a part of her everyday life? Do we love each other even when our projections of each other have been lowered? Are my negative experiences with my family of origin affecting our relationship? Can we work to heal together by getting good counsel? Do we have fun together? Do we communicate well? Do we fit together? These are questions that take time to answer. Do not rush in answering them.

Now that we have explored the different rules that came from the *I Kissed Dating Goodbye* culture and have seen some of the holes in them, it would be wise for us to come together as a community to create a new dating model. I'd love to see a revolution in the church in which we are allowed to date and have adult relationships and still maintain our values and boundaries, a revolution in which a man can feel like he can ask a woman out just to get to know her better without everyone in his life asking him when the wedding date will be. I'd like to see singles groups pop up in which men and women can talk in groups about topics such as communication, dating well, fears, and sex. I'd like to see groups that support the idea that single people need to learn about these things just as much as married people. Groups in which healthy dating practices are encouraged and taught by married people and single people alike.[43]

Maybe together we can create a culture that allows

people to date in healthy ways, ways that lead to decisions that are educated and safe. Perhaps we can get to a point where we feel safe to side-hug dating hello. (I would have said "kiss dating hello," but we've got to keep good boundaries, now, don't we?)

Chapter Thirteen

Hold the Ones You Love

"The most beautiful thing we can experience is the mysterious. It is the source of all true art and science. He to whom this emotion is a stranger, who can no longer pause to wonder and stand rapt in awe, is as good as dead; his eyes are closed." ~Albert Einstein

A few months ago I went to Washington to play a few concerts and visit my friend Carson. It was impossible for me to know as I boarded the plane that when I would get back to Colorado a month later (almost three weeks later than I had planned) my life would be turned upside down and I would see the whole world differently.

Carson has a very rare disease called Budd-Chiari syndrome, which is a fancy way of saying that his bone marrow produces too many blood platelets, making his blood too thick. It is a one-in-a-million disease, and he has an even rarer form of the disease, known as a JAK2 mutation, that was discovered only a few years ago.

The Bible says that "the life of every creature is in its blood" (Leviticus 17:14), and I have never seen this more clearly illustrated than in Carson's sickness. If his blood stays thick, it will clot and he could die, so he has to take blood thinners. But if his blood gets too thin, he will throw up lots and lots of blood.

Carson is a very inspiring person. He was diagnosed with Budd-Chiari eleven years ago, and despite all of his health problems, he lives every day well. I have never met anyone who has gone through so much suffering with their health; yet, I have never heard him complain. He makes a conscious effort to live every day in the moment, to remember the preciousness of life and the people around him. He knows it's possible that he won't have many moments left. Until his health recently worsened, in fact, he rafted and hiked and rock climbed. His favorite thing is "flying," his word for paragliding, which he has done all over the world.

Before he was diagnosed, Carson worked at a boy's home in Denver called Lost and Found. Soon he felt working at the facility was not enough; he didn't want only to be a mentor to these troubled kids. He wanted to be a father to them. He knew that someday he wanted to adopt.

After he was diagnosed, he still longed to take care of kids who needed a dad, but he also knew there was a possibility he could die. He didn't want to hold off doing foster care until he got married because he knew his days might be limited. He came up with a very unique solution: he started taking in older foster kids alongside his platonic friend, Trish, knowing that having two adults would be the safest way to care for the kids with his health problems. Carson and Trish have never been romantically involved nor have they ever gotten married, but they work and live together to take care of these kids.

One day, the state asked them to take in a three-year-old named Collin for a little while. Originally, Carson and Trish had agreed not to take younger children, but they had a peace about it this time and accepted. Even at such a young age, Collin had the biggest personality you could imagine, bringing laughter and joy to everyone around him. His older brother, Avie, who is so kind and wise that you have to remember that he is ten and not twenty-two, came to live with them a few months later.

Inevitably, Carson and Trish ended up loving these two brothers. Collin and Avie's birth mother really wanted the pair to take her sons. Carson and Trish were in a quandary: should they let these kids be put back in the foster care system, or should they take the boys as their own even though Carson could die?

The answer was clear. They loved the boys too much to put them back in the foster care system. So the state let them adopt the boys, fully aware that Carson and Trish were platonic friends. Theirs is a family like no other I've met, and their circumstances seem odd to people who don't know them well. But when you spend time with them, you realize that, despite the nontraditional nature of their family, those boys are deeply loved.

I had a very special week or so visiting Carson and Trish in Washington recently. But the sweetness ended abruptly when, one morning at 4 a.m., Trish came into my room and turned on the light. She asked me if I could take care of the boys as Carson had just thrown up a lot of blood and needed to go to the hospital.

The next twenty-four hours were a nightmare. At the first local hospital, Carson lost so much blood that they almost ran out of bags to transfuse. If the helicopter had come in any later to take him to Seattle, they would have run out and he could have died.

Trish and I stayed up all night looking at pictures of Carson and the boys, and the next day we drove to Seattle to see him in the hospital. When we got there, we walked into a room with three doctors and some other family members. They sat us down and very somberly told us that Carson would never see or talk to us again, but that he might be able to hear us. He was going to die in the next twenty-four hours, they said.

Sobbing, I called many friends to pray. Two people said, "Kate, you have been in this place before. Your nephew almost died when he was born, and you were on the road to dying or being severely disabled with Lyme disease. It is not a mistake that you were visiting this week. You are there for a reason."

My spiritual father, Chuck, told me, "You need to help Carson's family to take their eyes off of the problem and onto the goodness of God."

I marched into Carson's room, where he was unconscious and on a respirator that looked like a hockey mask. I don't know where I got the courage, but I went right up to him, grabbed his hand, and started singing songs over him. There were family members in the room who I had never met before who were probably wondering who I was, but I didn't care. I was going to worship God in the midst of this tragedy. I was going to speak life over him.

Carson's mom, Cheryl, had her head in Carson's lap and was crying. When I started singing, she looked up and started singing with me, even though she didn't know the words to the song. It was beautiful.

The doctors told Carson's family that they should tell him that it was OK for him to die, that Trish and the boys would be taken care of. I didn't want to go against his family or the wishes of the doctors, but I had a hard time doing what they had asked. So I woke up in the middle of the night and sang songs about life over him for about two hours, and I told him that he wasn't going to die. This is one of the songs I remember singing over and over:

> *I have a plan for you, I have a plan for you*
> *It's never too late, it's never too late*
> *It's not too late for you*
> *I have a plan for you, I have a plan for you*
> *It's going to be wild, it's going to be great*
> *It's going to be full of me*[44]

I told Carson that he was going to see Avie and Collin get married and that he was going to meet his grandkids. Even writing such a strong encouragement now is difficult because I know Carson still has many complications. I didn't (and don't) want to give false hope, but when I said those words to him I could clearly see him in a chair with all of his grandkids around him, telling stories. There was hope in that hospital room that night—a hope so tangible that I could almost touch it. When you are at someone's deathbed, you stop taking that person for granted. The wonder and mystery of Carson lay in that bed. The threat of losing him made me remember how precious he is, how precious my life is.

The next morning, Carson started to stabilize. He could motion to us, indicating that he was semi-conscious. The doctors were practically in shock. They had been sure that he would die, saying that they had never seen anyone with insides like his. He had lost almost every drop of his blood in twenty-four hours. How could he possibly be waking up? they wondered aloud.

Friday was the day he was supposed to die. By Monday, he was eating and sitting up. He even walked into the waiting room, still attached to his IV, to surprise all of us. He waved at the nurses and the doctors as he walked by, and they looked at him in disbelief. They had thought that his name wouldn't have been on the door by the end of the previous weekend, and here he was walking around.

Wednesday of that week was Avie's birthday. Carson cleaned up, got his hair cut, and put on some new clothes. We hung balloons all over the ICU waiting room, and we bought pizzas, cake, and gifts for Avie. We invited the doctors and nurses and loved ones of the people in the ICU to the party. A place of despair had become a place of hope and laughter.

The boys had been told that weekend that Carson, their father, was going to die. But now they knew there was still hope. When the boys arrived at the hospital, Avie and Collin waited at the end of the hallway for their dad to come to them. He walked toward them. I remember it in slow motion. When he got to them, he threw his arms around them and started sobbing. Their reunion was one of the most beautiful moments that I've ever seen.

At the end of the party, Carson went to every person in the room, even people he had never met, kissed them on the cheek and told them that he loved them.

I stayed with Carson and his family for two and half weeks in the hospital. We would spend at least ten hours a day there. Every day I called as many people as I could think of to pray, and I was on the phone for hours at a time. There are few times in my life when I have felt so loved. People all over the world prayed for Carson. Friends who had never met him would cry with me on the phone. Because his life was dear to me, his life was dear to them.

I wrote two songs for Carson while I was with him in the hospital. The first was about him flying, about how beautiful it was to see someone in the midst of the sorrow of disease choose to live with joy. My favorite lyric is this: "You have taken your sorrows and turned them into wings." That line captures who he is. After I sang the song for him, some of his doctors and social workers asked me to sing it for them. They all started crying when they heard it, not just because of how beautiful the song was but because of how beautiful Carson's heart and story was.

I also wrote a song for him and his family. These are some of the lyrics:

> *When all is said and done*
> *Sometimes we forget how precious life is*
> *Until it's nearly gone*
> *So hold the ones you love*
> *Hold the ones you love*
>
> *I will not take for granted*
> *How life surrounds me like air*

From this day forward
I will hold the ones I love
Hold the ones I love

And oh, how precious life is
And oh, how precious life is

You realize both the beauty and the difficulty of life when you are in a hospital. Everything that is bad in the world gets magnified, and everything that is good in the world gets magnified. Life feels so precious. Life feels so hard. Everyone around you seems beautiful, but everything around you seems tragic. As Steven Galloway said in his book *The Cellist of Sarajevo*, "It's a rare gift to understand that your life is wondrous, and that it won't last forever."[45]

When I finally came home to Boulder while Carson waited for a liver transplant, I was in a state of wonder for a few days. I almost kissed the kind grocery clerk on the cheek, and I wanted to give the homeless woman begging on the street a huge hug. I wondered why anyone would fight with each other, why every day was not a day that we would celebrate the beauty in one another.

David James Duncan writes that

> Wonder is unknowing experienced as pleasure. Wonder is a period at the end of a statement we've long taken for granted, suddenly looking up and seeing the sinuous curve of a tall black hat on its head, and realizing it was a question mark all along. Wonder is anything taken for granted—the old neighborhood, old job, old buddy, old spouse—suddenly filling with

mystery. Wonder is anything closed suddenly opening [. . .] I believe it is wonder, more than courage, that conquers fear of death.[46]

Carson got a liver transplant a few weeks after I left and was able to get out of the hospital on Christmas day. He still has complications, so we can all remember to keep praying for him. But he is alive. It seems that his wonder—even more than his courage—has conquered his fear of death. The doctors told us that they have seldom seen anyone survive something like what he went through. The world has been given a gift because Carson is still alive.

Carson's story teaches us an important lesson about our relationships, especially those of our close family members and the spouses and children we may one day have. The lesson is this: normal life—nondeathbed life—is what we live most days. We often take people for granted. In a very literal way, we think that our loved ones are granted to us. That they are in our possession and that we will never lose them. Instead of remembering how precious someone is, we forget. Instead of focusing on the mystery of the essence of a person, we focus on the fact that the trash has not been taken out. Instead of remembering every right thing that someone has done, we remember every wrong thing. We forget and we forget and we forget.

Recently, while on my quest to gain wisdom from married couples, I sat down with my friends Matt and Amanda. I asked if they had any advice for me. Matt answered, "When I first married Amanda, it was my

commitment to talk about her in a positive light. This
didn't mean that I couldn't be honest and process my
marriage with friends. It just meant that I committed to
saying loving things about her when she was was in the
room with me and when she was somewhere else. After
a while, though, I learned that talking about Amanda
positively was not enough. I needed to commit to *seeing*
her positively, too. She is such a beautiful person, and if
I don't choose every day to see that, I will take her for
granted. Now I make a conscious effort to notice her
uniqueness and beauty every day."

Like Matt, I want to posture my heart toward seeing
the beautiful. I want to make a commitment in my heart
to remember. If I do ever get married and on the occasions when romance is lacking and there are children and
bills and mundane-ness, I want to look at my husband
and see the mystery of who he is. I want to call to mind
all the kindness and complexity and commitment and
laughter and looks and caresses and beautiful history that
are wrapped up into this person that God has given me.
I want to be aware that this person is not merely granted
to me, but that there are limited days in his life and that
I should appreciate the gift of the days I spend with him.

For today, even before I am married, I have dear
friends in my life who are also mysteries. They have
laughed with me over meals and cried with me over
breakups. Each person is so precious. I want to remember.
Even though I am no longer in the wake of a near-
death experience, there are still people on the street who
are lonely, like that homeless women who needed a hug.
Maybe this time, I should just hug her.

I also want to remember that there is a God who cannot be contained by eternity and who listens to me every day when I pray. There is one who sees me beautiful, who doesn't take me for granted. He created universes that I can't begin to understand, but he also created a leaf with tiny lines on it that I can hold in my hand. That's how personal he is. I don't want to take him for granted, either. Looking at him for one moment would change my life. It would take a lifetime to fully take in one tiny part of him. That's how full of wonder he is.

Life is precious. The people in my life are precious. My God is precious.

Help me remember, Lord. Help me remember.

When all is said and done, sometimes we forget how precious life is until it's nearly gone. So hold the ones you love. Hold the ones you love.

Chapter Fourteen

Pity Parties and Prodigals

I would like to devote this chapter to an important ritual that single people practice: the pity party. I have been the event planner for quite a few of these festivities, so I can talk about them with some expertise.

Okay, I'll stop being modest and just and say it: I am the Martha Stewart of pity parties.

Here are some of my pity party planning tips:

1.) Come depressed. Your goal should be to obsess about how crappy your life is and to have your guests comfort you as you talk about how crappy your life is.

2.) Be selective about who you invite. Don't include people who will say things like, "Get over yourself" or "It's time to move on." They will ruin everything.

3.) Wear the proper outfit. This usually includes glasses, pajamas, and rabbit slippers.

4.) Plan your menu. I like to have potato chips as my

appetizer, Ben & Jerry's as the main course, and maybe another kind of Ben & Jerry's for dessert. An assortment of deep-fried foods works great for side dishes. If you want to get especially fancy, add a garnish of marshmallows and Tootsie Rolls.

5.) Prepare your music. Mood music is very important! I have a mixed tape labeled "Kate's Songs that Allow Her to Wallow in the Depths of Despair." This tape contains such classics as

"All By Myself," made popular by our mentor, Bridget Jones.[47]

"Against All Odds" by Phil Collins. You cannot get a more apt song for a pity party than one that contains lines like "How can I just let you walk away, just let you leave without a trace? There's nothing left here to remind me, just the memory of your face," and the best pity party line ever: "You're the only one who really knew me at all." Classic.[48]

"Baby Got Back" by Sir Mix-A-Lot. Wait, how did that get on here?[49]

6.) Plan some really fun games! My favorites are "Pin the Tail on the Ex-Boyfriend" and "Hit the Piñata that Looks Remarkably Like Someone I Used to Kiss."

7.) Make sure to light lots of candles. If the pity party goes well, you and your guests can use them to burn your love notes and pictures. For a more memorable finale, build a bonfire and have everyone bring their own pity party memorabilia to throw into it. That way you can wallow in heartache as a community. What a great way to bond!

8.) If you want to provide party favors, I can hook you up with some nice pity party T-shirts. I have soft gray ones that you can wear to bed, hot pink ones with sparkles that come in sets of three for when you go out with the girls, and light blue ones that have "Pity Party" very subtly written on them that are especially nice to wear to church. I also have pity party mugs and pity party signature Kleenex.

Follow these tips, and you, too, can have a great (read: pathetic and soul draining) pity party!

In all seriousness, the reason I am such an expert is that I have thrown many pity parties lately. In fact, these pity parties grew to a climax when my long-time counselor recently challenged me to examine what I would do if I never got married and didn't have biological children. How would I rearrange my life if my only choice in having a child were to adopt? She also asked me if I thought that my life would still be valuable if I never had a traditional family. It was very difficult for me to say yes.

I was devastated after this counseling session. I felt really sorry for myself, but I also recognized how much my thoughts about remaining single and childless have consumed me lately. I haven't been sleeping very well. My mind has been mulling over my difficult childhood, wondering if it contributed to a man not falling in love with me. I have been bitter toward ex-boyfriends for rejecting me. I have been doubting God's goodness and even his existence because he has not given me this, one of my deepest desires.

In other words, I have been trying to blame anyone I can for my pain.

This difficult counseling session helped purge the deep sadness in me, and it also made me realize that I am spiritually "hung over" and exhausted from all the pity parties I have been throwing for myself.

In the midst of all these revelations about myself, I read a passage in the Bible that depicted someone who threw one of the best pity parties in the New Testament: the older brother in the story of the prodigal son.

In this well-known and wonderful story, we see a family with two sons: the young, rebellious son and the elder, religious son.

The younger son demands his share of the estate from his father and leaves home after his father complies with his request. In that day, it was an act of disdain for a son to demand his inheritance before his father died. Essentially, the younger son says to his father, "All I want from you is the gifts you can give. I don't want your love; I want your loot."

After the younger son leaves and lives a life of debauchery, he sees that his life away from home is nothing like he expected it would be. He squanders his money and becomes poor and lonely. He is hired to feed pigs and craves even the pods that the pigs are eating. In his hunger, he realizes that even the servants in his father's house had never been as hungry as he was. He recognizes that he has a good father and that it was his own selfishness that got him into his place of need.

He decides to go back home, but because of the way he left, he has no hope that his father will welcome him back as a son. He truly believes that the only way his father would take him back is if he were to return home as a slave. He even creates a speech to give his father at his return:

"'Father, I have sinned against heaven and
against you. I am no longer worthy to be called
your son; make me like one of your hired men.'
So he got up and went to his father" (Luke
15:18-20, NIV).

In one of the most beautiful illustrations of love in scripture and in any other literature, the father sees his son
coming from afar and gives up all his dignity by running
out to greet the young man as he walks the road home.
The father throws his arms around his son and kisses him.

The younger son tries to deliver his speech, saying,
"'Father, I have sinned against heaven and against you. I
am no longer worthy to be called your son.'

But the father says to his servants, "'Quick! Bring the
best robe and put it on him. Put a ring on his finger and
sandals on his feet. Bring the fattened calf and kill it. Let's
have a feast and celebrate. For this son of mine was dead
and is alive again; he was lost and is found.' So they began
to celebrate" (Luke 15:21-24, NIV).

Notice that the father doesn't even let the younger son
finish his planned speech. When the prodigal son tells him
he is not worthy to be called his father's son and is about
to tell him to make him like one of his slaves, the father
interrupts him with sentiments of total acceptance, offering
symbols of sonship and calling him "son."

That's what the Father of mercy does. He doesn't even
let us finish our sentence when we are talking about
coming to him as a servant. He shatters our mindsets of
slavery with the power of extravagant love and calls us his
children.

The second part of the story, however, the part that I have often overlooked, focuses on the older brother. Let's read on:

> Meanwhile, the older son was in the field. When he came near the house, he heard music and dancing. So he called one of the servants and asked him what was going on. "Your brother has come," he replied, "and your father has killed the fattened calf because he has him back safe and sound."

> The older brother became angry and refused to go in. So his father went out and pleaded with him. But he answered his father, "Look! All these years I've been slaving for you and never disobeyed your orders. Yet you never gave me even a young goat so I could celebrate with my friends. But when this son of yours who has squandered your property with prostitutes comes home, you kill the fattened calf for him!"

(See! The older brother even rivals me with his pity party skills!)

> "My son," the father said, "you are always with me, and *everything I have is yours.* But we had to celebrate and be glad, because this brother of yours was dead and is alive again." (Luke 15:25-31, NIV, emphasis mine)

I have read the story of the prodigal son many, many times. I've heard dozens of sermons on it. I've written songs about it. It is one of my favorite stories in the Bible. But at the same time, I have often had a hard time relating to the young son.

You see, I've been pretty good most of my life. I haven't run away from my Father's house, nor have I squandered my inheritance. As a modern celibate, I certainly haven't had much loose living. I have lived in my Father's warm home since I became a Christian at sixteen years old. I've loved living here. I've never really wanted to run away.

But after my counseling session, I realized that, though it was hard for me to relate to the younger son, I could deeply identify with the older son. Like him, I have been bitter at God for not giving me what I wanted when I worked so hard for him.

In the parable, the older son stays in his father's house throughout his brother's rebellion. He works the fields for his father. He acts more like a slave than a son.

As I contemplated the story from the perspective of the older brother, I suddenly saw the passage as if it were a movie.

I saw the father, after his younger son ran away, grieving the loss of this son and longing for comfort and connection with his older son. However, the older son slaves away in the fields day after day. After a hard day of work, the eldest son comes home for dinner, sits at the far end of the table, and barely talks to the father. The father wants to talk to him, but the son refuses. He passes his father in the hallway and the father longs to hold him, but the son just brushes past and goes to his room, wallowing in his self-made prison. All he can do is think about what he does for his father, how hard he works, and how his father does not give him enough. He does not believe that his father is a good father.

Then, the prodigal son comes home. But when this joyous occasion takes place, the older son is working in the fields. He misses the homecoming, the running, the laughing and crying, and he misses the party. His work has separated him from the intimate workings of his family, from the celebration of their life together. Even when he finally gets to the party he refuses to go in. He throws his own party of pity, so he misses the party of joy.

When he finally gets to talk to the father about his anger at the situation, he says something to this effect: "I have slaved for you all these years. I have given you everything. But you have not given me anything. Nothing."

There are many times when I have acted like this older son. There have been times when I have wondered why, when I have served my Father my whole life, he has not answered my most consistent prayer: the prayer for a family. Forget this whole grace thing. I want God to see my good works and reward me for them.

Sometimes, in the deepest places of my soul, I do much more than throw a pity party. I become bitter. I start to wonder if my Father is really a good father.

As Henri Nouwen says:

> Returning home from a lustful escapade seems so much easier than returning home from a cold anger that has rooted itself in the deepest

corners of my being. My resentment is not something that can be easily distinguished and dealt with rationally. It is far more pernicious: something that has attached itself to the underside of my virtue.[50]

Nouwen is right. It is difficult to come home to the Father when I consistently allow this cold anger inside of me. When I consistently allow thoughts like, "I have tried every day of my life to live for you. I have given up a lot to do so. Why, then, am I still not married? Why would you throw other people a party and forget me when I have been faithful to you for so many years? Are you even the good God that you say you are?"

Here is the real question that I need to ask myself: Is it God who is not good, or is it my perspective that is not good?

Look at this story. The father is the definition of a good father. And yet both sons feel like the only way they can be loved is to be his slave.

This good, good father never wanted slaves. He wanted sons. When he addressed each one of them, he specifically called them both sons. In both the case of the rebellious son and the case of the religious son, the father wants to run to them crying out, "My child. My child! You've come home to me!" He wants to lavish his love on them, spinning them around until they are dizzy with his love, falling down with them, laughing. He wants to cover them with accepting kisses and celebrate their return. Whether they have been living off scraps from a pig sty like the younger son, or living off grimy, bitter thoughts like the older son, he wants to give them a loving home to come to at the end of a long, hard journey.

Now and forever, everything he has is theirs. They don't have to steal his inheritance. They don't have to slave for his inheritance. They already have it.

This is not the picture of a bad father. It is the picture of the most loving father that has ever lived. The father's heart was never wrong. The sons' perspectives were wrong.

My perspective is wrong.

The other day, a mentor of mine said to me, "Kate, I want you to focus on trusting God during the next few months."

I sounded like a recovering Pharisee when I said, "But I do trust God!"

She answered very gently, "No, Kate. No, you don't."

I realized almost automatically that she was right. The anxiety that I had just spilled out to her indicated how little I trusted him. When it comes down to it, I don't always see him as good. In my heart, I often don't believe that God will give me a good life. Sometimes I believe that even if he is good, I will negate his blessings if I don't make the right choices.

This, my friends, is the life of a slave. This is the life of someone who does not trust her Father.

If I were to tear through these cobwebs of disbelief and really listen to my Father speak to me, he would respond in the same way that he responded to the older son.

"My child," he would say, "*all that I have is yours.* You think that I am withholding from you. If I could lift up the veil of your limited perception, you would know what a good father I am. You would know that there is nothing I have that doesn't belong to you."

I know what you are thinking because I have had similar thoughts: "OK, Kate. You say that God is good and that everything he has is mine. But there is one thing you have overlooked. I still don't have a family."

I know. I don't totally get it either. But I am learning slowly that I don't just want the Lord's loot. I want his love. I don't want to go to God just because I want something. I want to go to him because I love being with him.

One of my favorite psalms says, "I have stilled and quieted my soul; like a weaned child with its mother. Like a weaned child is my soul within me" (Psalm 131:2, NIV).

I first saw this psalm on a placard someone gave me. The placard, however, did not have the word "weaned" on it. It's not really a Christian bookstore kind of word, so it was left out.

One day, I asked the Lord why the word "weaned" was in the psalm. I felt like God told me that it was because a weaned child doesn't come to its mother for milk anymore. The child comes because she loves being with her mother. She chooses to be still and quiet in her mother's arms. In that moment, she doesn't need anything else but her mother's embrace.

I don't understand why I'm not married. I don't understand why there is poverty or slavery in the world. You may not understand your divorce or your being fired or your being sick. You may not understand the disappointments in your life. We may never understand those things in our lifetimes.

But I want to choose to still and quiet my soul. I

want to choose to go to my Father even when I don't have answers to my questions. Even when, in my limited perception, I think he is holding out on me. I need to let go of trying to figure it out and I need to rest.

Henri Nouwen says,

> I am beginning now to see how radically the character of my spiritual journey will change when I no longer think of God as hiding out (or holding out) and making it as difficult as possible to find him, but instead, as the one looking for me while I am doing the hiding. When I look through God's eyes at my lost self and discover God's joy at my coming home, then my life may become less anguished and more trusting.[51]

The Father reaches out to us.

He says, "I never asked you to be a slave. All I ever wanted was for you to be my child. I have been looking for you for a long time. You don't have to hide behind your good deeds, behind your broken dreams, behind your bitterness. Come, eat at my table. When you pass me in the hallway of our house, let me give you a hug. Come rest here in my arms.

All I have is yours.

My peace is yours.

My hope is yours.

My passion is yours.

My friendship is yours.

My heart is yours.

My kingdom is yours.

My family is yours.

Most of all, my love is yours. You have it now. You will never lose it. You just have to believe it that it's there."

The cover of my last album is very special to me. It is a drawn picture of a girl who looks like me. She is in a shabby room. She is wearing rags. She is looking into a mirror. In the mirror is an image of the same girl, but she is dressed in a gold and purple robe. There is a beautiful light surrounding her and flowers at her feet. She reaches her hand towards the poor version of herself on the other side of the mirror, a look of compassion and love on her face.

Often people miss this little detail, but on the wall, there is a small framed picture. It is a picture of the same girl in her rags, running toward a man in a purple and gold robe.

Her father.

This picture beautifully depicts that the homecoming of the prodigal son (or the prodigal daughter) is not the end of the story. If we will let our Father embrace us, the memory of him running fervently to welcome us with open arms is something that will stay with us forever. It is a picture that we will frame and hang on our walls. It will become one of our most precious possessions, whether we are staying in a palace or in a dingy, tiny room.

After we have been embraced by God, when we look in the mirror, we will not see someone in rags, bitter and torn. We will see ourselves as the Father sees us. Beautiful. Compassionate toward ourselves and others. We will see ourselves wearing his robe, wearing his identity. We will no longer be slaves but beloved children.

The way that we see God will change everything, even the way we see ourselves.

I realize now that pity parties are all right every once in a while because they allow me to express my pain, but God wants to throw me a much greater party. A life-changing party. One that makes my thoughts of bitterness fall to the wayside. One in which my Father clothes me with the robe of his mercy, the cloak of his joy. One in which I am the honored guest.

A party that celebrates that I have come home to him.

How to Live Life Well

1.) Love God.
2.) Love the person standing in front of you.

Chapter Fifteen

How to Build Your Own Family
Part I:

Giving Yourself to Others

When I tell people I am writing a book about being a single Christian, I inevitably get into conversations with them about relationships. If they are also single Christians, we usually end up telling our sob stories and our success stories. We talk about our fears about getting older and our frustrations with not having a family. We comment about how it seems like Christian guys would rather clean every bathroom in Grand Central Station with a toothbrush than ask us out on a date because of the pressure they feel to get married too fast.

Etcetera, etcetera, etcetera.

Even when I am not talking to other people about my love life or lack thereof, I am infinitely more aware of it than usual because I have had my heart broken pretty badly in this season. I have been saturated with thoughts about my own loneliness. And now, after months of thinking about it, I am not just lovesick; I am sick of love. Of thinking about love. Of talking about love. Of reading about love. Of writing about love. Most of all, I am sick of thinking about myself.

In the book *Singled Out*, John Stott says,

> The greatest danger [singles] face is self-centeredness. We may live alone and have total freedom to plan our own schedule, with nobody else to modify it or even give us advice. If we are not careful, we may find the whole world revolving around ourselves.[52]

In other words, as singles, it is really easy for us to become self-absorbed.

In fact, I have become really self-absorbed.

It is in selfish seasons like this that I wrongfully believe that I have no choice over whether I have a family or not. While it is true that I can't get a husband the same way I can get a degree, I do have some control. The catch is, what I could have at this point is not the husband-and-kids-and-white-picket-fence family that I expected to have. Instead, I can make the choice to build my own, beautiful nontraditional family. And there is no better way to do this than to put myself in situations in which I can love people who desperately need love.

A good example of this is found in the life of my friend, Jude Tiersma Watson. Jude grew up as the child of Dutch immigrants. She worked overseas for a season and then, twenty-four years ago, she became a missionary with InnerCHANGE. Each of those twenty-four years was spent in the Latino slum apartments I mentioned earlier in the book. Jude is a missionary to the people in this poor community, and she is also a professor at Fuller Theological Seminary. You don't often imagine professors living in slums, but that is the life she has chosen.

Jude realized early in her singleness that she didn't want to pine away for a life she didn't have. She felt like she might want to get married at some point, but she wasn't obsessed with finding her husband. She refused to spend her life waiting, so she dove into an interesting, rich life by moving into a very poor neighborhood in order to bring the love of Jesus.

Jude was still single into her late thirties, but she wasn't that worried about it. She didn't feel the aching loneliness many of us struggle with because she had chosen in her twenties to build her own family. Her brothers and sisters and sons and daughters in this nontraditional family helped fulfill her innate desire to give and receive love.

When Jude was thirty-nine, she unexpectedly met her husband, who was interning with InnerCHANGE. He was African American and eight years her junior, but they didn't let that get in the way of the love they knew God had for them. They never had any biological children, but they spiritually adopted a Latino girl who had grown up in the same apartments the couple lived in.

The daughter of Dutch immigrants marrying an African American man and adopting Latino children? This was probably not the life Jude expected! But it is so much more colorful and deep of a life than she ever imagined.

Like Jude, I want to stop being so self-absorbed in my own season of singleness. I want to remember the lonely and brokenhearted not only because it will make me feel better, but also because God himself commands us to care for the poor and the downtrodden and the abandoned.

A few years ago, I did an exercise that shook me out of my self-absorbed bubble and made me realize how deeply God cares about the poor. I was listening to a teaching on biblical justice by Rob Morris, founder of Love146, a wonderful organization that fights sex trafficking. During the teaching, Rob had listeners flip through their Bibles for ten minutes and look for verses about taking care of the poor, helpless, or hurting.

I opened to a psalm but figured that I should move on to another book, since the Psalms probably wouldn't have much about taking care of the poor. But one of the first verses I read was Psalm 41:1 which says, "Blessed is he who considers the poor; the Lord will deliver him in time of trouble" (KJV).

I flipped a few more pages, thinking the first one was a fluke. Then I read "He has given freely to the poor, his righteousness endures forever" and "He raises the poor out of the dust, and lifts the needy out of the ash heap" (Psalm 112:9, NAS and Psalm 113:7, ESV). Then, "I know the Lord will maintain the cause of the afflicted and justice for the poor" in Psalm 140:12 (NAS).

Those were just a few of the many verses I read. By the time the ten minutes had run out, I had come across dozens of verses about helping the poor. It was mind-blowing to me.

Let's try that same experiment here. Set this book down for a moment and pick up your Bible. Flip through it and, with no help from concordances, mark down all the verses you find about taking care of the poor. Do it for ten minutes. Write down all of the references. After the ten minutes is up, ponder what you read for a while, breathing deep and listening to God's heart.

What kind of verses did you find? Was it easy to find them? My bet is that they were everywhere you looked. Those verses are all over the Bible—there are around two thousand of them.

Since I did that exercise, I have noticed verses about taking care of the poor constantly. I couldn't believe I hadn't seen them before. I mean, I knew that Jesus talked about the poor, but not like this. I didn't see that it was on his mind all the time, that loving the poor and those who have no family was one of the passions of his life.

If the God I love talks about this topic so many times, shouldn't I make it a focus of my life, as well? Shouldn't I care about it because he cares about it?

I don't want to be like Thomas Jefferson, who took his Bible, cut out every verse he didn't like, and glued all the other passages together. I don't want to pick and choose the parts of the Bible that will convince me that the world revolves around me and my pain.

Understanding how much Jesus loved the poor was

what drove me to work with kids on the street and inner-city kids. When I walk side-by-side with people in this way, I glimpse what it would be like to build my own nontraditional family.

I loved sitting across the table from my street friends, laughing and crying with them as if we had been companions for years.

I loved going to the music class I taught and talking to Star, with his toothless grin and his six-foot-five hugs that immersed me in love. He cried every time I sang and would say, "I don't understand why I do that. Why do I cry every time you sing?"

I loved having Roach tell me his life story before I recorded one of his rap songs, I loved seeing him weep uncontrollably when we prayed for him, and I loved hearing him tell my teammate "you're the best friend I have in this city."

I loved receiving email messages from Jack, my favorite street friend, who recently turned himself in to the police and served a stint in prison because he was getting serious about walking with God and he felt like turning himself in was the right thing to do. The morning of my writing this chapter, I found this in my in-box: "If no one today has told you that they love you, give me a call. Because I will tell you." I need someone in my family to tell me that some times. The fact that it is a street friend who tells me that, someone who seems so different than me, makes it all the more beautiful.

As Mother Teresa put it, "If we have no peace, it is because we have forgotten we belong to each other."[53] Let's remember that we belong to each other. Let's love other people enough to remind them that we belong to each other. Maybe then we would finally have some peace, even if we don't have the traditional family we always wanted.

I know there are a million causes that want your resources. A million different ministries vying for your attention. It can be overwhelming to hear all of the statistics. Sometimes you don't know where to look. You don't know if you can make a difference, so you don't look anywhere. You look away.

But behind these causes are real people with real faces and real voices and real senses of humor and real tears. People like the girls in Love 146's safe homes. People like Jack. People who you can really help. People who can really help you.

My advice for you is to prayerfully choose one of these causes and be passionate about it for the rest of your life. Learn about your cause. Introduce yourself to the people who are behind that cause. Find out what you and your friends can do to make a difference. Don't just feed at a soup kitchen; come out from the serving line and sit and eat with the precious people you have served. Don't just give money to an organization that fights sex trafficking; find out how to write to the kids in the safe home and get to know them. Shane Claiborne says in his book, *The Irresistible Revolution,*

> What our world is desperately in need of [is] lovers, people who are building deep, genuine relationships with fellow strugglers along the way, and who actually know the faces of the

people behind the issues they are concerned about.[54]

When you get to become friends with people who are hurting, they almost always end up bringing beauty to your life that you never expected. You realize that, whether homeless or orphans in Uganda or your mean boss, they are not that different than you are. You all want the same thing: family.

Getting to know people causes your priorities to change. You would rather comfort them and be comforted by them than saturate your own life with comforts that are not attached to human beings, or to be saturated by your own disappointments.

If all you think about is love and your lack of it, try to gather up the courage to walk out the door into a world that can be cold, a world that might have pain in it. But a world that is beautiful. A world where you will truly be alive. A world where you might even find a family.

To sum up this chapter, let's look loving the ones around us through the eyes of two very different men: Buddha and Jesus.

As Frederick Buechner says,

> Buddha sits enthroned beneath the Bo tree in the lotus position. His lips are faintly parted in the smile of one who has passed beyond every power in earth or heaven to touch him. "He who loves fifty has fifty woes, he who loves ten has ten woes, he who loves none has no woes," he has said. His eyes are closed.

Christ, on the other hand, stands in the garden of Gethsemane, angular, beleaguered. His face is lost in shadows so that you can't even see his lips, and before all the powers in earth or heaven he is powerless. "This is my commandment, that you love one another as I have loved you."[55]

In essence, Buddha says that if you don't love as many people, you won't have as much pain. And he's probably right. It's hard to love people. The reward of self-absorption is that you will be very comfortable. But you will also be very alone.

Jesus, on the other hand, says to love, love, love, love, no matter how hard it is, no matter what you have to give up. He tells us to passionately love, as he has passionately loved us. Passionately love our friends, our spouses, our children, our enemies, the poor.

Love even if we have to die for it. Because that is what he did.

Jesus was never absorbed by himself. He was never absorbed with avoiding pain. He was always absorbed by his desire to love.

Chapter Sixteen

How to Build Your Own Family
Part II:

Living in Intentional Community

In the last chapter, we talked about building your own family by focusing your energy on something other than your singleness, like loving the poor. In this chapter, I want to look at another way to build your own family: intentional community.

Last year I moved to California to be in ministry school for a season. A friend had hooked it up for me to live on a farm with four other single girls. I had never met the girls before, and I had butterflies in my stomach when I drove onto Shiloh Farm that first day.

Soon after introducing themselves to me, my four new

housemates said, "We are doing something this weekend, but you don't have to join us if you don't want to."

I said, "No, I'd love to join you!"

They said, "Well, you really don't have to join us."

And I said, "No, I'd love to!"

And then they said, "We're slaughtering chickens."

That was the weirdest icebreaker I had ever heard of.

"I'm in," I said.

I figured that if I were going to be eating those chickens, I should at least help get them to my plate. I won't get into the grisly details about that weekend, but let's just say that we had farm-fresh organic chicken for dinner a lot that year and that I now know how to use a machete.

We knew the chickens would taste wonderful in all of their organic, nongenetically-modified glory, but their little bird legs were spread out in a way that made it obvious they did not come from the store. We stuffed the chickens for flavor, and, with their sprawled-out legs, the poor chickens looked like they were giving birth to lemons.

I got to know some unique animal friends while I lived there on the farm. There was the chicken that I liked to call Pet Cemetery. She had somehow hurt her neck, and so her head was turned almost completely around to face behind her. As a result, she slowly walked backward instead of forward. It was totally creepy.

We also had Peg Leg, a rooster who had lost his leg when a horse stepped on it. My roommate, Kristy, fastened a popsicle-stick prosthetic onto the nub, but it didn't help. Peg Leg just figured out how to get around on one leg. I frequently saw him hopping around the farm. He was definitely the ladies' man of the farm despite his disability. I now understand the term "cocky" in a whole new light.

And then, there were the bunnies. We tried hard to decide what to do about our rabbit problem. The rabbits were nuisances. They destroyed our garden, so we knew we needed to find a way to get them off the farm. When we found a bunch of tiny babies in our tool shed, we figured out exactly what to do: We brought them into the house and let them hop all over our beds and sleep with us because they were so cute.

Captain Jack Sparrow became one of our favorite bunnies. He was black with white spots. My four-year-old nephew John Mark would come visit and loved feeding carrots to that little bunny. To this day, every time I visit John Mark he asks me where Captain Jack is. I tell him that he got married, moved to Los Angeles, and became an accountant with a nice mustache.

People would often ask me if someone else ran the farm, having a hard time believing that four girls would want to do that. But those four were very unique girls.

The four friends had moved out to California together from Cairo, Illinois. In Cairo, they had all met at a prayer ministry in a very poor, 90 percent African American community, and eventually, they decided to come to California to go to school. These girls were such close friends that I can almost guarantee that they will be friends for the rest of their lives.

When I moved in with them, I soon learned that they were intentional about community. We shared all of our food. No permanent marker labeling was allowed. People often think that sharing food is a strange thing to do in a roommate situation, but isn't sharing food what a family does? I didn't have as much money as the other girls had during that season, so I couldn't contribute as much as they did. They didn't care. They didn't keep tabs.

Every weeknight one of us would cook dinner for everyone else. Even if we didn't have time, we *made* time to do it. We sat at dinner and talked about our days. Afterward we would often sit in the living room and talk more, processing our hopes and disappointments and dreams. There was always a lot of laughter and love in that house.

It ended up being a very hard year for me with a breakup and a major struggle with depression. I was so thankful to have the girls on the farm around me during that season. The longer I was there, the more I realized why I loved living with them so much: Even if they were not a traditional family, they were a family, and they allowed me to be a part of it.

All the girls at Shiloh Farm were incredibly special, but I want to focus on Kristy for a little while. At forty-two, Kristy was a little bit older than the other girls. I often talked to her when I needed wisdom, and she always had some to offer. A month or so after I moved in, I asked her if it was hard for her to be unmarried and with no children at her age. That's when she let me know for the first time that she felt called to a life of celibacy. She wanted to be devoted to the Lord and to loving the people around her without being married, and she was totally at peace with that.

During our conversation, Kristy said something that I have thought about quite a bit since then. She said, "Even though I've been called to a life of singleness, I know that I don't want to be alone. I know that I will choose to live in intentional community for the rest of my life."

I learned that she was the one who started the prayer house in Cairo. The intentionality of that community was no mistake. She valued community, and so she worked hard to create an environment that worked toward that goal. With the help of her friends, she had not only built a ministry, she had also built a family.

(On a side note, one day I was talking to a classmate who had a male friend in his forties who also felt called to celibacy. Without even thinking about it, I said, "Oh, my gosh! I have a roommate named Kristy who is also in her forties and celibate and she is wonderful! We should set them up on a date!" My friend looked at me as if I were crazy, and I realized I had just said one of them most ironic things ever.)

Recently I moved back to Boulder, Colorado, where I'm originally from, to write this book and pray about my next steps in life. I get along well with the girls I live with, and they are very respectful, but we don't see a lot of each other. We have different schedules, and we are hardly ever at the house at the same time, except to sleep. In other words, it's like most roommate situations in America.

I have been thinking a lot about the contrast between my two recent roommate situations, and I have been realizing how much I love living in intentional community.

It is hard to come across intentional communities like the one at Shiloh Farm because our society has often sacrificed community for comfort.

Case in point: My friend Matteo went to Italy, one of the most family-oriented cultures in the world, a few summers ago. He noticed two major differences between the way of the Italians in the little town where he was living and the way of the Americans he was used to. First, he noticed that the Italians ate meals together (mostly at home) every day. Second, he noticed that the Italians walked everywhere. The people in his village understood that eating meals together and walking places were too important to give up, no matter how busy life became. They knew that conversations happen around tables and on street corners and around food that takes time and effort to cook. The people understood that slowing down to eat and to walk does not just nurture the body, but that it also nurtures connection. It brings about family.

Connection does not happen so much when you are eating frozen dinners in front of the TV. But at least we are comfortable there, right?

From my experience, this is the world most Americans have created to keep ourselves as comfortable as possible: we wake up and turn on the radio so we don't have to think. We eat our cereal alone so we don't have to cook. We drive to our jobs so we don't have to interact. We nod to our roommates when we get home so we don't have to invest. We put fences up so we don't have to connect. We do social networking so we don't have to communicate anything deep. We check our iphones and laptops as often as possible to saturate our minds with information so we don't have to contemplate. We watch our televisions so we don't have to feel. And in these days that blur into months that blur into lifetimes, we are incredibly comfortable. But we are also incredibly unhappy and lonely.

David Janzen, in *The Christian Community Handbook*, discusses the idea that the convenient invention of the car changed the community life of America forever. He writes,

> This American life is a life dispersed: we work
> ten miles away with people who live twenty
> miles beyond that, buy food grown a thousand
> miles away from grocery clerks who live in a
> different subdivision, date people from the other
> side of town, and worship with people who
> live an hour's drive from one another [. . .]
> There is little sense of consonance, commit-
> ment, spontaneity, or stability in this paved new
> world. Because there is so little overlap in our
> different spheres of life, there is little chance
> for our socializing, creativity, or service to be
> spontaneous. The nearest things to spontaneous
> occasions in the fragmented lifestyle of suburbia
> is the persistent stream of texts, tweets, and
> status updates on our cell phones.[56]

My point in this chapter is not to rail on America. My
point is for us to acknowledge the fact that we are a part of
a society that has often traded in community for comfort
and that we should be aware of the consequences of that
trade. If we want to foster community, we are going to
have to make a conscious effort to go against the flow of
our fast-moving and convenient environment. We are going
to have to give up some of our comfort in order to create
a space for love.

How do we do this? By taking time in our days to eat
with people, even if doing so is inconvenient. By planting
a community garden that our neighbors can share. By

stopping by a friend's house to bring them a gift. Small things make a big difference. But what is, in my opinion, the best way to go against the flow of our non-spontaneous culture? Create an intentional community in which you live with other people in order to foster family life.

One of my favorite films in which the character discovers the joy of living in community is *The Visitor*. In it, the main character—an older man named Walter—lives in a house alone in Connecticut. He hates his job as a professor. His wife, who was a classical pianist, died, so we find him taking piano lessons in order to remember her and fill his empty days. But he doesn't enjoy it.

Walter owns another apartment in Manhattan. When he visits his apartment on a business trip, he is surprised and furious to find that there are two illegal immigrants, Tarek and Zainab, living in his second home. The immigrant couple had not meant to steal Walter's home; they had rented the apartment from a swindler who had pretended to own the apartment.

At first, Walter is angry and demands that the couple leave his apartment. But, due to outside circumstances, he is convinced to let them stay there for a while, and slowly he and the couple develop a close friendship. Walter learns to play hand drums from Tarek, the husband living in the house. In one of my favorite scenes, Walter, who is a straight-laced business man, runs from his office during his lunch hour to join a drum circle with Tarek at the local park. There is such joy on his face as he plays drums in his business suit. Indeed, through his relationship with the immigrant couple, Walter discovers who he is and what he loves.

After many months of the three of them living together, the couple faces the threat of deportation, and Walter fights hard to keep them in the United States. You can see how much he loves them; they have now become the family that he longed for.

We would do well to follow in Walter's footsteps. We would do well to move beyond our lonely, convenient lives in order to build our own families. I would love to see a movement of singles who are committed to having a family even if they are still looking for a spouse or if they have decided to remain single. Maybe these singles might even choose to live together, make meals together, dream together, like the girls at Shiloh Farm.

You can be in a family if you want to be. You don't have to be alone. You can build your own family. Certainly, living in intentional community takes commitment and letting go of some things you love—like some of your independence, like making sure there is not a spot on the countertop, like having to talk to and listen to people who you may not always like, like taking the time to eat and laugh and share life together, like pulling yourself away from your Facebook page. It might take you having a vision and sacrificing to make it happen.

Personally, I would rather have covenant than independence. I'd rather make meals that take time and effort with my friends than eat a bowl of cereal, go to my room, and watch YouTube videos alone. I'd rather have a house that is full of love and companionship with a few dirty dishes in the sink than a perfectly ordered, spotless house with no one in it.

I'd rather have family.

It's not good for us to be alone. No matter how much freedom we have when we are alone, it is not good. God himself said that.

It *is* good for us to be in a family, even if we have to build our own.

Chapter Seventeen

Thirty, Flirty, and Fertile

Recently, my roommates (all of whom are over thirty and single) and I went to a '90s-themed roller skating party. At first we couldn't think what to wear, so we decided to look online for inspiration. As we glanced over the images that were a result of our search, many bad fashion memories came back to us. The Jennifer Aniston haircut. The little plastic circle that you could slip onto your T-shirt to make it almost look like you tied it, but not quite. The hat with the big sunflower on top that could have come right off the show *Blossom*.

My roommate, Amanda, decided to play the part of the early '90s girl. She was quite *Saved by the Bell*-esque, wearing florescent clothes with funny patterns and overly-teased bangs. My other roommate, Jess, decided to go for the mid-'90s-grunge look, complete with a morose spirit hanging over her that was obviously inspired by Pearl Jam.

When cheery early-'90s Amanda saw gloomy mid-'90s Jess, she tried to lead her to the Lord. She said, "Jesus can lift your spirits AND your hair!"

Jess dressed the part perfectly: cotton leggings, Converse, and an oversized flannel shirt. But the little detail that pulled it all together was a black velvet ribbon choker with a cross hanging from it. Jess parted her bangs down the middle, put some black makeup around her eyes, and wore frosted lip gloss.

At first I was amused when I saw her outfit. It looked just like what I wore almost every day when I was in college.

Then I got a little freaked out.

THAT LOOKS JUST LIKE WHAT I WORE ALMOST EVERY DAY WHEN I WAS IN COLLEGE!

What? How could this be? How could I be having flashbacks of my high school and college days while getting ready for a decade theme party?

I started counting backward. It's been twenty years since the early '90s. TWENTY YEARS? I remember my mom going to a "Remember the '60s" party when I was growing up. And now that was me! The '60s are twenty years from the '80s, and now the '90s are twenty years from today. Is it possible?

I had to sit down on the bed for a moment to calm myself down. Then I put on my florescent orange shirt and big black boots, applied a ridiculous amount of hairspray, and headed off to the party.

I got even more freaked out once we got there.

This roller skating joint had not been redone since the very decade we were celebrating. Or if it had been, it had been redecorated to look like every single roller skating place I ever went to when I was in middle school. Orange carpet. Disco balls and lights that put patterns on the dance floor. Brown roller skates that have dangerously long orange shoelaces. (Doesn't anyone even test those roller skates? There are children wearing these things, for heaven's sake!) People going at very high speeds who suddenly swerve around the gateway on the verge of crashing, flashing a smile at you to cover up the fact that they were about to knock six people over. Couples holding hands. Awkward people inching very slowly along the walls, trying to pretend they have some semblance of balance. The inevitable game of Crack the Whip, where a line of people hold hands while skating around the circle, forgetting the unfortunate people at the end of the line who are going so fast they could at any moment be propelled against the wall.

When I ventured onto the rink, I wondered if anyone was watching me. I was quite cognizant of the way I smoothly ran my wheels across the floor, of how hot I looked in my one-sleeved shirt, of how all the 25-year-old guys there probably had no idea that I was in high school in the '90s because I still looked so young and vivacious. But those thoughts all stopped abruptly when my too-long shoelaces got caught up in my wheels and I fell flat on my face.

Just like in middle school.

It was as if I were at this party in the past and the present at the same time. It was tripping me out almost as much as my too-long shoelaces were tripping me up.

After I brushed myself off and started another lap, my

ears tuned in to the music that was playing.

Even. More. Freaked. Out.

I know "Ice Ice Baby" was from the '90s. It seems like it belongs in the '90s. The same goes for MC Hammer and "U Can't Touch This." But what about "Mr. Jones" by Counting Crows? "Semi-Charmed Life"? "One Headlight" by The Wallflowers? It does not seem like fifteen-plus years since I first heard those songs.

I came home from that party feeling pretty old.

People say to me all the time, "Well, age doesn't matter. It's just a number."

You know what my response always is?

"Tell that to my uterus."

My uterus and I have had quite a few problems in our relationship as of late. In truth, my uterus is pretty frustrated with me.

The argument she has with me all the time sounds like this: "Kate, what am I good for if I don't house a little baby for nine months? I've been sitting down here for thirty-some years with nothing to do! I need a job, Kate! Go out there! Find yourself a man! Get married and get these eggs fertilized."

I feel sheepish and guilty every time my uterus and I talk. Because she's right. I do need to "get out there." But it's more complicated than it seems. I try to tell her that, and she says, "Why didn't you go out with all those guys who liked you ten years ago? Why were you so picky?"

"I don't know, Uterus. Life only makes sense in the rear-view mirror." That's what I always say. Or maybe that's a country song. Either way, it's true.

According to the social norms, my uterus and I have

exactly three years, eight months, and eight days to get ourselves pregnant.

That is the day I turn forty, the day my eggs shrivel up and die. Forever. If they do—by some monumental miracle of God—get fertilized after that day, my babies will supposedly look like a cross between Jay Leno and Steven Tyler.

At least that's what the people around me and society have told me.

I asked my last boyfriend if he had ever thought about adopting. He was eight years younger than me, mind you.

"Well, I hadn't really thought of it before," he said. "But I have since I started dating you."

"Why?" I said.

"Because you're thirty-three. You can't have children anymore, can you?"

"What?" I asked. "Of course I can! I have six years, three months, and twenty-two days left, thank you very much!"

If you look at these quotes from some of the aforementioned chick flicks that have now been emblazoned in my head for many, many years, you'll understand better what I'm talking about.

In *When Harry Met Sally*, Sally is thinking about the fact that she is still unmarried while talking to her friend Harry, and exclaims, "And I'm gonna be 40!"

"When?" Harry responds.

"Someday!"

"In eight years!" Harry says.

And here's the clincher from Sally—the thing that reveals her fears: "But it's there! It's just sitting there like this big dead end."

A big dead end. Not the most positive picture of

mid-life painted by our darling Meg Ryan.

In *Bridget Jones's Diary*, Bridget Jones is asked why there are so many single women in their thirties. She responds, "I guess it doesn't help that we have scales under our clothes."

In *Sleepless in Seattle* a friend says to Meg Ryan's character, "It's easier to get killed by a terrorist than to find a husband after the age of forty."

Meg responds indignantly, and her friend retorts, "That's right; it's not true. But it feels true."

When we look at the messages in these movies, I wonder if we have valid reasons to be afraid of hitting middle age without a family or if we just live in a culture that is freaked out by the number forty. What are the facts here?

Well, it is true that it is a bit riskier to have babies after forty. But it is far from true that one is more likely to be killed by a terrorist than to have a baby after forty. Women often have perfectly healthy babies at an older age. Plenty of celebrities have had babies over forty: Jane Seymour, Emma Thompson, Susan Sarandon, Madonna, Cheryl Tiegs (twins at fifty-two!), JK Rowling, Geena Davis, Meryl Steep, Helen Hunt, Halle Berry, Nicole Kidman, Mariah Carey. Shall I go on?

Friends of mine who are midwives have told me that they have had many clients in their forties—and even fifties—who have had healthy children. One of my midwife friends, who lives in Portland, says the majority of her clients are over forty.

And if an older woman cannot or does not want to have biological children, she can choose to adopt. I have always wanted to adopt. Even when I was in college, I would tell people that if I found out I couldn't have children, I would simply take in a child that didn't have a home. I don't think I would be devastated if I found out I could not have children of my own. There are plenty of children who desperately need a loving family, and I would love to give it to them. I have even considered adopting as a single woman if I get into my forties and am still not married.

Almost every time I see multiethnic families, I feel so drawn to them that I figure my longing must be a stirring from the Lord. Every time I watch a movie about a teacher reaching out to hurting teenagers—especially in the inner city—it is inevitable that I cry through the whole movie. I don't know if that means I will adopt inner-city kids or if I will just work in the inner city loving them. But I do know that either way, I want to be a big part of these children's lives. I want to love them well.

"OK, Kate," you say. "You've made a good argument. Maybe it's not as bad as I thought to have babies or to adopt after forty. But I don't want to be in a wheelchair and on oxygen when my kid graduates high school."

I know. I feel the same way. But I also want to wish away the fact that "Only Wanna Be With You" by Hootie and the Blowfish came out in 1995. I don't like getting older, but I am getting older. I can choose to be angry at my reality, or I can choose to accept it and make the best of it.

There you go. There's my two cents. Just ignore the culture. Just adopt. Just accept reality and move on somehow.

I want to admit something to you. I am sitting in my arm chair right now on a Thursday afternoon, reading over the paragraphs I just wrote. I am realizing that I've been covering up my fear with my author hat, leading you to believe that I know all the answers.

The truth is, I am just as scared as you are. Really, really scared. So now I'm going to tell you what is actually going on inside of me.

I joke about my uterus and about roller skating parties, but the truth is, when I can't sleep at night I am probably laying awake thinking about the fact that I am getting older and might never do all the things I dream of doing, especially having a family.

There are things I love about getting older. I feel comfortable in my own skin. I have overcome a lot and have become a much wiser human being. I can make strong decisions, I communicate well with the people I care about, and I love who I am, all of which were distant desires ten years ago.

But there are other things that I hate about getting older. I cringe when people ask me how old I am, especially men whom I am attracted to. After I read that even older men look for women under thirty-five, I have seriously considered faking my age on dating websites. Lately I have avoided being around children, simply because it makes me so sad that I might never have my own. I wake up some mornings not wanting to have to go through the day because it means getting older. I have a birthday coming up this weekend. I am forcing myself to celebrate, but really, I want to cry every time I think about it.

At my age, I don't have a lot of choices in my dating

life. On the rare occasion I do get to go on a date, my fear often kicks in. I try desperately not to be desperate. If I am not careful, I end up wearing my biological clock on my sleeve. I all but stand up on the table and do an interpretive dance of the old DC Talk song "Time is Ticking Away," complete with my arms moving to the rhythm like a clock.

My memories are starting to feel farther and farther away, which really frightens me. I wonder if my life has meant anything. I feel pressure to find more meaning in life because time is slipping away so fast.

So there it is. The honest truth. I am scared to death. And if you get down to it, I am scared *of* death. Of getting older and dying without doing all that I was supposed to do.

One of my greatest fears is that I'll get older without having a family, and the only way I can possibly get over this fear is to trust God. Yes, I am scared, but I need to believe that if God wants me to have a family, I will have a family. He has no time constraints. Nothing is too difficult for him. On the other hand, if I don't have a family, I will be OK. I can still choose to live a beautiful life.

I refuse to let my belief in the goodness of God rest on whether or not I have a family. There are some things that I will never understand, and this may be one of them, but I will keep on believing in the goodness of God.

In Ecclesiastes 3:10-11, Solomon gives us these words: "I have seen the burden God has laid on men. He has made everything beautiful in its time. He has also set eternity in the hearts of men; yet they cannot fathom what God has done from beginning to end" (NIV).

Let's look at this verse a little closer. You read the first part—"I have seen the burden God has laid on man"— and, if you are like me, you wonder, "What is this mysterious burden that God has laid on men? To have to work to provide food and shelter for your family? The evil in the world? Mosquitos? The Kardashian sisters?"

The next sentence identifies the great burden that God has laid on us, and it surprises me.

Here is the burden: He makes all things beautiful.

Why would God making something beautiful be a burden? That sounds much more like a blessing doesn't it?

Read on and you might understand: "He makes all things beautiful *in its time*." The great burden is not that he makes all things beautiful. It is that he makes all things beautiful *in its time*, in ways that are beyond our limited perception.

Sometimes I get angry at his timing. I do not like getting older. I don't like that our memories of roller skating are getting farther and farther away. I "cannot fathom what God has done from beginning to end." Standing within the walls of time, I don't understand.

But do you know what verses precede the one about God making all things beautiful? They are very familiar verses. I'll give you a hint: The words of the verse may have been played at my Mom's "Remember the '60s" party.

There is a time for everything, and a season for every activity under the heavens:

> a time to be born and a time to die,
> a time to plant and a time to uproot,
> a time to kill and a time to heal,

a time to tear down and a time to build,
a time to weep and a time to laugh,
a time to mourn and a time to dance,
a time to scatter stones and a time to gather
them,
a time to embrace and a time to refrain from
embracing,
a time to search and a time to give up,
a time to keep and a time to throw away,
a time to tear and a time to mend,
a time to be silent and a time to speak,
a time to love and a time to hate,
at time for war and a time for peace
(Ecclesiastes 3:1-8, NIV).

There is a season to everything. A time for everything. Everyone's story and everyone's rhythm is different. Not one is better than the other.

My friend Sam said to me the other day, "Kate, do you realize that if you had a child a few years ago, he or she would most likely have had Lyme disease? Maybe it was not God withholding from you when he didn't let you have a baby at that age. Maybe it was his grace. Maybe he wanted to wait for you to be healthy to let you have a child." It had never occurred to me before that my having to wait might not have been God stealing something, but him waiting to give me something much better.

We can't often see things clearly from our limited perception. Perhaps God stands above us, above time, as if we were in a parade, and he throws down love on us, like floating ticker tapes. He throws down love from that lofty window, seeing the bigger picture, and we don't understand what he is doing from beginning to end. But the love still falls down on us, surrounding us as we march on, unaware.

Thank you, Jesus. Thank you for your grace. Whether I have a husband or not, whether I have children or not, and even when I don't understand your timing or my disappointments, I can trust this one thing: you make all things beautiful.

Chapter Eighteen

The Deepest Love Story

A few years ago, a dear friend of mine took a class on myths. In it, he learned stories from different cultures and religions around the world and saw so many common threads that he began to doubt whether any of them were true. He wondered if the story he grew up with—the story of Jesus—was just another myth.

My friend came away from that class pretty sure that none of the stories, not even the Jesus stories, really happened.

I have thought a lot about his experience, and what I have concluded is that the similarities between myths do not suggest that none of the stories are true, but instead that there is one root story. The Great Love Story from which all other stories flow.

The deepest, most beautiful love story.

I don't think there could possibly be a deeper story than

the one I believe in. Since this book is about love, I want
to explore this mysterious story. Though you might have
heard it many times, I want you to try to hear it as if you
were hearing it for the first time.

It goes like this:

Once upon a time, there was a God who was so blin-
dingly beautiful that when he spoke, stars would come
forth. When he walked, life would spring up everywhere.
When he breathed, love would pour out of him like water.
He did not simply have hope and love and passion living
within him; he *was* hope and love and passion. He was
light, and darkness could not live in the light.

He was love and love must be shared, so he breathed
into dirt and his image became a man. From the beginning of that man's life, God wanted to give him the
greatest gift: the gift of intimacy, of oneness. So he gave
Adam himself, and he also gave Adam a counterpart, a
companion.

The counterpart was called woman, and the two were
made as one.

From the very beginning, God did not want slaves; he
wanted a family. He gave the two a choice: they could
turn their backs on him or they could run toward him.
Their power to choose reflected that they were made in
God's image. God set before them death and life, blessings
and curses, the knowledge of good and the knowledge of
evil.

They chose to turn against him.

Because darkness cannot live in the light, God was
separated from his beloved, and his heart was broken.

We who have had our hearts broken may think that we

are the only ones who have faced the pain of unrequited love, but our God has suffered through it like no one else ever has. Sometimes, when I struggle with rejection, I ask God, "Have you ever gone through this?"

God's answer? "Every day."

In *The Divine Romance* by Gene Edwards, the author explores the unrequited love that God had for his people in the Old Testament.

> He had stood there all morning [. . .] watching intently toward the south. Finally, in the late afternoon, it began to appear, first as a tiny speck on the horizon, gradually growing until it became a moving sea of humanity. It was *his* people, lately set free from slavery [. . .] he stared at this moving mass of humanity until the image before him blurred and began to change in form and, finally, became one person. His eyes now saw not a multitude of people, but only a lovely young girl, coming up from Egypt, crossing the hot sands and moving toward him [. . .] Again and again he issued forth to her a cry:
>
> > *Return to me.*
> > *Return to me!*[57]

There are many stories in the Old Testament that give imagery to God's broken heart toward this girl. One of the most poignant is the story of Hosea.

God asks his prophet Hosea to marry a prostitute

named Gomer. Hosea does so, and Gomer ends up having affairs with other men and prostituting herself even while she is married to him. The book's language is often disturbing, full of pain, frustration, and anger. However, behind all of it is God's deep, groaning desire for his loved one to come back. He longs for his counterpart—his beloved—to return to him.

As a foreshadowing of what was to come, God says to Hosea, "Go, show your love to your wife again, though she is loved by another and is an adulteress. Love her as the Lord loves the Israelites, though they turn to other gods [. . .] So [Hosea] bought her for fifteen shekels of silver" (Hosea 3:1-2, NIV).

Did you catch that? *He bought his wife back.*

Imagine what Gomer the prostitute went through when her husband bought her back. She chose to sell herself to men who abused her and destroyed her self-worth rather than to stay with a good man who loved her deeply and tenderly.

Can you picture the scene? She is standing in the local square, peddling herself to the highest bidder. She is dirty and bloody from the men who have beat her and have treated her as if she were their property. Hosea steps in front of her. She sees him and is ashamed. This is the only man who has ever truly loved her. The only man who has given himself to her instead of taking from her. The only man who has seen her for who she and still loves her, even in her brokenness. But she has left him. She has forsaken him. How would he ever want her back?

In this scene, she is wearing the garments of a harlot, and she is exposed. Hosea sees Gomer in all of her sin. Is he going to yell at her and make a public spectacle of her like she deserves? Is he going to beat her for leaving him? Will he stone her for her unfaithfulness, which would be completely acceptable in that day?

He does none of these things. Even though he is her husband and has rights over her, he shows her how deeply he loves her. He shows her that she is valuable to him. Astonishingly, Hosea walks up to the man who currently owns his wife and hands him his money. He picks his wife up into his loving arms, kisses her, and carries her home.

These are the words that God speaks to his beloved:

> Therefore I am now going to allure her; I will lead her into the desert and speak tenderly to her. There I will give her back her vineyards, and I will make the Valley of Achor ["trouble"] into a doorway of hope. There she will sing as in the days of her youth, as in the days she came up out of Egypt.
>
> In that day, [. . .] you will call me *my husband.* You will no longer call me *my master.*
>
> I will betroth you to me forever; I will betroth you in righteousness and justice, in love and compassion. I will betroth you in faithfulness, and you will acknowledge ["intimately know"] the Lord.
>
> I will show my love to the one called *"Not my loved one."* I will say to those called *"Not my*

people," "You are my people;" and they will say,
"You are my God" (Isaiah 2:14-16,18,19-20,23,
NIV, emphasis mine).

In that day he will change our name from "abandoned"
to "loved," from "orphan" to "the one with a home."

The story of Hosea wasn't just a love story between
one man and a prostitute. It was the story of one God
and a world that had turned against him, a world that he
longed to know intimately again.

After centuries of God's wooing and his beloved
rejecting, the day finally came for the mystery of the
world to be revealed. The day when he would reconcile
his beloved back to himself.

The God of the universe, the God who cannot be
contained by eternity, made himself small. So small, in
fact, that we could hold him in our arms, close to our
hearts. He was a child named Emmanuel, which means
"God with us." This incarnation is, in itself, a mystery
beyond understanding.

That child grew up to be a man. Far from being a
weak man, as he is often depicted, he fought for the
rights of the poor, the rights of the outcast. It seemed
that the more people hated these "sinners," the more
Jesus loved them, much like Hosea loved the prostitute so
many years before. Jesus spoke identity and worth into
those the world deemed worthless. He saw them like no
one else had seen them; he loved them like no one had
loved them.

As my song "Mary's Song" says,

You called out my name
It's like I heard it for the first time.
I was wretched and ashamed
But you saw me like no one has seen me.

You said "You've had many lovers
Who love themselves when you are near
But I alone have known you
And I love you like no one has loved you."

I said, "I am broken I have nothing left to bring."
You said,"Vessels must be broken to pour out an offering."
So I pour all my tears out and I bend to kiss the feet
Of the one who sees me lovely
The one who sees me beautiful[58]

God's love for us and the new names he gave us came with a price, though. To truly see us holy, to completely see us beautiful, he knew that he had to eradicate the darkness and tear down the walls between him and his people.

He knew that laws couldn't bring us back. We would never be holy enough to approach him. The only answer was to pay our punishment for us, to buy us back like Hosea bought back his wife. And so, he gave up his life. The most precious commodity on earth, the blood of God himself, was poured out to purchase us. That's how valuable we are to him.

He hung on that cross like a "lamb slain before the foundations of the world" (Revelation 13:8, Aramaic Bible in Plain English). He did not just hang on a hill called Calvary, he hung above eternity, above time.

In *The Road to Daybreak*, Henri Nouwen talks about his

time at L'arche, a home for mentally handicapped adults. One Good Friday, all of the handicapped people and their workers gathered together. He and the other priests took down the cross that hung behind the altar and held it so that everyone could come touch it.

As he stood there with his beloved handicapped friends, Nouwen pictured Jesus with his arms open over a world filled with great suffering:

> Imagining the naked, lacerated body of Christ stretched out over our globe, I was filled with horror. But as I opened my eyes I saw Jaques, who bears the marks of suffering in his face, kiss the body with passion and tears in his eyes. I saw Ivan carried on Michael's back. I saw Edith coming in her wheelchair. As they came—walking or limping, seeing or blind, hearing or deaf—I saw the endless procession of humanity gathering around the sacred body of Jesus, covering it with their tears and their kisses, and slowly moving away from it comforted and consoled by such great love [. . .] With my mind's eye I saw the huge crowds of isolated, agonizing individuals walking away from the cross together. Bound by the love they had seen with their own eyes and touched with their own lips. The cross of horror became the cross of hope, the tortured body became the body that gives new life; the gaping wounds became the source of forgiveness, healing, and reconciliation.[59]

This is what Jesus did for us on the cross that hung above the world. He met us in our suffering.

As Jesus hung suspended over time, war, disease, pain, divorce, poverty, and hell itself were driven into him, and they were immersed in his all-encompassing love. The angels flew to the end of history; they captured suffering and sin and threw it on him. This happened beyond time. That is why we have victory over darkness even now while we suffer on the earth.

The final thing that Jesus took upon his tortured body was death itself.

And then, the veil of the temple was ripped in two. It was no longer just the high priest who could approach God face-to-face once a year. Now, all people had access to him. We see a representation of this beautiful picture when two people are married and the bride wears a veil. The moment after the covenant is announced, the two are asked to kiss. The veil is lifted. In essence, the bride says, "Up to this point, I have not made myself completely vulnerable to you. You have known part of me, but you have not known all of me. I lift this veil because now is the time for love. I am making myself completely vulnerable to you. Vulnerability means risk and pain, but ultimately, it means intimacy."

When Jesus spread his arms open on that cross, he made himself completely vulnerable. At any time, we can crawl into his arms that are spread wide in vulnerability. At any time, he can hold us.

But this is still not the end of the Greatest Love Story.

One day, one glorious day, a wedding will take place. The bride that God fought for throughout all history—the one he gave his life for—will finally come.

Again from *The Divine Romance*:

> A door opens in the new heavens [. . .] the
> New Jerusalem. A city of a hundred million
> shining stones, each glowing with the glory of
> the light that is its center. And the center is the
> Lord, Christ Jesus!
>
> The city begins its decent, and, as it does, it
> begins to change. A galaxy of living light is
> swirling downward in the skies. Gradually
> the stardust of light becomes a multitude of
> people—the vast host of the redeemed, the
> multitude no man can number.
>
> The brightness grows, the lights become all
> one. At the center of this light, a form begins
> to emerge.
>
> Standing before them is the Bride of the Lamb.
>
> Her eyes have never seen or known one
> glimpse of the tragedies that befell her in the
> old creation. She stands there in the strength
> and perfection of youth. Her glowing visage
> tells a thousand tales of love, of passion, of
> singular devotion to her Lord.
>
> The woman begins to glow with a brightness
> for beyond the ends of belief. The glory of the
> brightness of the Lord ignites with a fire that

immerses, and then consumes all else.

Forever! No more alone.[60]

This is the deepest love story. The story from which all other stories flow. Whether we know it or not, this the story that we live in.

In the end, it will not really matter if you are single or married or divorced, if you are beautiful or ugly, if you are abandoned or cherished.

You are the Beloved.

Forever, no more alone.

Afterword

You are stronger than you think you are.

You, your hands dirtied with the soil where you till up the rocks of generations gone by. Your tears watering the ground, making the roots grow deep and wide while you are unaware. You labor, you dig, you claw this tiny piece of land where others buried their dreams and gave up trying.

But not you. You keep going. You never give up. You see the tree in the seed, and you will fight until that tree is standing before you, it's long willowing arms grasping your hope in its branches.

You are stronger than you think you are.

You, covered in all your scars. Where your face was grazed with false imaginings that you were not beautiful enough. Where your hands were caught in fields of cotton when you didn't believe you were free. Where you were marked across your chest the day you thought that they left because you weren't worth it. Look closely, love. Look closely because those scars are gilded with gold. Those scars have become your crown.

You are stronger than you think you are.

You, dancing there with your face against the wind. Not a pretty dance, but a wild dance. A hold on for dear life to the hope dance. An I will never stop believing in your goodness dance. A shake the sadness off your skin dance. You, with your feet pounding against the ground to the rhythm of your unsurrendering spirit. With your knees soiled and bleeding from the prayers and the longings and the times you almost gave up. With your arms thrown up in surrender and beckoning and awe. "You are my love!" you yell, "And I will never stop believing!" There is burning against your back as you lift up your face, because your wings are returning, love. Your wings are returning.

Look at me and believe now. You are stronger than you think you are. Stronger than you think you are.

THANK YOU...

First of all, I want to thank my editor, Laurie Thornton (www.lauriethornton.com). You worked almost as hard on this book as I did. You are brilliant, and you are also a good friend.

To my wonderful tough-love counselor, Dana Robinson. It would have been fair for me to put you as a co-author of my book since so much of the wisdom on these pages came from you. Thank you for guiding me so well through the last five years. (To check out Dana's absolutely beautiful reflection and renewal center, go to www.thedesert-sanctuary.com).

To Mom and Dennis, Shawn and Celeste, Will and Marie, Neal, Kai, Dax, Ariel, Jeremiah, Arowyn, and my sweet sweet John Mark. We went through a lot this year, and I am glad you are my family.

To my dear friend Becca Bundy for being a sounding board for this book and for listening to so much of the pain and joy that are depicted in these pages. Seven years and I can't think of one time that I didn't love being around you.

To the many women in my life who have brought joy and purpose to me. Aimee Herring Brewer, Kate Kemp, Shauna Lott, Dee Butcher (one of the most faithful people I know), Emily Malloure, Joanna Howard, Sanyu Majola, Andrea Weeks, all my High School Girls, the Tetrapees.

Special thanks to Shauna for brainstorming with me on the cover and Aimee for the brilliant name.

To Aaron Strumpel (www.aaronstrumpel.com) for walking with me through so many journeys and for globe-trotting the world with me. You are a good, good friend.

To the Louisville Pirate Bikers: Trace, Matteo, Kelsey, Kelly, Casandra, Glad and Scotty, Jenny, Aaron, and Trung. Over the years you have brought me so much happiness and so many Irish drinking songs.

To Carson Stitt. I want to live a better life because of the way that you live yours. You have inspired me so deeply, beyond words.

To the whole Stitt and Nilles family (including Collin and Avie!) for accepting me as family when most people would have politely asked me to leave.

To Roger. You always make me laugh so hard and I miss you!

To my entire Bread of Life family, especially Chuck and Linda Parry. I miss you all so much, especially every Thanksgiving and Fourth of July. Some of the best moments of my life were spent with you. I looooove yooooou!

To Access, especially Ryan Taylor. You have brought so much depth to this season of my life. Thank you.

To Origins Community. I love you all so much. There is no place I'd rather be on a Sunday night than with you.

To Luke Flowers (www.lukeflowers.com) for always doing such an amazing job with my artwork and for being a wonderful encouragement every time.

Thanks To Amy Calkins (www.aurora-pub.com) for her meticulous editing, proofreading, and generosity.

Thanks to Caleb Seeling at Samizdat Creative (samiz-datcreative.com) for publishing this book, which freed me from having to go with some big company that was going to rip me off. I literally thanked God when I realized I could work with you. I am thankful that we share similar passions and that you made a way for the book to finally become a reality.

To all my supporters over the years for helping my dreams become a reality, especially Den and Grace Nichols, Mom and Dennis, Marcia Talvite, Garth and Kirsten Schultheis, Cathy Little, First Covenant Church in Vero Beach, FL, Mark and Jan Mckinnies, Jody and Louise, so many others. It brings tears to my eyes to think about what you have done for me.

To the many organizations that have challenged me to live a life beyond myself, especially InnerCHANGE (www.innerchange.org), iempathize (www.iempathize.org), AIDchild (www.aidchild.org), and love146 (www.love146. org).

ENDNOTES

1 *Wikipedia*, s.v. "Old Maid," accessed November 22, 2012; and Jim Linderman,"Old Old Maid Cards and an Old Old Card Game" (blog), Dull Tool Dim Bulb, accessed on November 22, 2012, http://dulltooldimbulb.blogspot. com/2009/11/old-old-maid-cards-and-old-old-card.html#. UK6En47Txid.

2 Some information for this section was found in *Wikipedia*, s.v. "The Game of Life," accessed November 22, 2012.

3 Eric Klinenberg, Going Solo: *The Extraordinary Rise and Surprising Appeal of Living Alone* (New York: Penguin Press, 2012)

4 urbandictionary.com, s.v. "white man's dance," accessed June 12, 2012.

5 These dance moves and more can be seen on Youtube at http://www.youtube.com/watch?v=2HiuCaaQhxg.

6 Linda Lyons, "What Frightens America's Youth?" *Gallup.* com (March 29, 2005), http://www.gallup.com/poll/15439/ what-frightens-americas-youth.aspx.

7 Don Chaffer, "The Worst Is My Being Alone," *You Were At The Time For Love* (1999).

8 Kate Hurley, "Hey Little Girl," *Sleeping When You Woke Me* (2007). Find the album at katehurley.com or on iTunes.

9 Kate Hurley, "You Are Not Alone," *Sleeping When You Woke Me* (2007).

10 Kate Hurley, "Joy Comes In The Morning," *Weak and Strong at the Same Time* (2010).

11 *Alcoholics Anonymous: Big Book* (Alcoholics Anonymous World Services, Inc., 2001).

12 If you are sick with anything that you have a hard time diagnosing or that you are not getting better from, it is worth going to see Dr. Shauna Young in Durango, CO (assertivewellness.com). She has cured people of Lyme, cancer, autism, and many other diseases.

13 Deborah Fileta, "Marriage Does not Solve Your Problems," *Relevant* (May 23, 2012), http://www.relevantmagazine.com/life/relationship/features/29263-marriage-doesnt-solve-your-problems.

14 Melody Notkin, "My Secret Grief: Over 35, Single and Child¬less," *Huffington Post* (January 12, 2002), http://www.huffington¬post.com/melanie-notkin/my-secret-grief-over-35-s_b_1202808.html.

15 The section on Hannah was inspired by a teaching given by Ray Hughes. Learn more about Ray at selahministires. com.

16 Kate Hurley, "Love of My Life," *Sing Over Me* (forthcoming).

17 Kate Hurley, "I Have Overcome," *Sing Over Me* (forthcoming).

18 "Dolls," *This American Life*, Episode #153, NPR (March 3, 2000).

19 David Colman, "The Unsettling Stories of Two Lonely Dolls," *The New York Times* (October 17, 2004).

20 Dare Wright, *The Lonely Doll* (New York: Houghton Mifflin Company, 1957).

21 "Dolls," *This American Life*, Episode #153, NPR (March 3, 2000).

22 Steven Pressfield, *The War of Art: Break Through the Blocks and Win Your Inner Creative Battles* (New York: First Black Irish Entertainment, 2002).

23 These are the plots of the films *When Harry Met Sally*, *Sleepless In Seattle*, and *You've Got Mail*, respectively.

24 Hara Estraff Marano, "The Expectation Trap," *Psychology Today* (March 3, 2010).

25 Henri Nouwen, *The Wounded Healer* (New York: Doubleday, 1975).

26 Graham Cooke, "The Inheritance," YouTube video, 8:33, posted by "Deni Huttula," August 17, 2007, http://www.youtube.com/watch?v=dEisSxR2cps.

27 Henri Nouwen, *Seeds of Hope: A Henri Nouwen Reader*, edited by Robert Durback (New York: Doubleday, 1997). Italics mine.

28 Thomas Merton, *No Man is an Island* (New York: Houghton Mifflin Harcourt, 2002), 168.

29 As quoted in J. John and Mark Stibbe, *A Bucket of Surprises* (London: Monarch, 2002).

30 As quoted in John Hayes, *Sub-merge* (Ventura, CA: Regal Books, 2006).

31 A more in-depth account of this inspiring story can be found in John Hayes, *Sub-merge*.

32 Wes Bridel, "First-born: Birthright and Inheritance," Kingdomcalling.com (June 20, 2009), http://www.kingdomcalling.com/2009/06/29/first-born-birthright-and-inheritance---part-2.

33 David Wilkerson, "Jabbok! A Place of Total Surrender," http://www.tscpulpitseries.org/english/undated/tsjabbok.html.

34 C.S. Lewis, *A Grief Observed* (New York: HarperCollins, 1989).

35 Donald Miller, *Searching For God Knows What* (Nashville: Thomas Nelson, 2010).

36 "This is Your Brain on Love," *Radiolab*, NPR (August 28, 2007).

37 Danny Silk, "Covenant in Relationship," YouTube video, from a teaching given at VerticalCall on December 4, 2001, posted by "ELIatVerticalCall," May 17, 2012, http://www.youtube.com/watch?v=Aj9rryTbbhc.

38 Dann Farrelly, "Brave Communication," http://store.ibethel.org/p1992/brave-communication.

39 This definition of "helpmate" is discussed in more detail by Bill Johnson in his teaching "Transformed People Transform Cities: Being A Bride" (disc 6), which you can find at http://store.ibethel.org/p4771/transformed-people-transform-cities.

40 "Star-Crossed Love," *This American Life*, Episode #308, NPR (February 10, 2006).

41 This observation and others like it can be found on the web¬site thingsaboutlove.com, http://www.thingsaboutlove.com/what-does-love-mean.

42 "Young, Free, and Amish." YouTube video uploaded by "NationalGeographic" as part of "Amish at the Altar" on October 26, 2010, http://www.youtube.com/watch?v=5lKlBPdgA_E.

43 I attended a group called the Single Life Workshop for a year, and it was a great model for exactly this kind of singles group. Our small groups were co-ed, and we talked about very deep issues like pornography and sexual abuse as well as things like being good communicators. Find out more about bringing groups like this to your own community at singlelifeworkshop.org.

44 United Pursuit Band, "Come Away," *United Pursuit EP* (2008).

45 Steven Galloway, *The Cellist of Sarajevo* (New York: Riverhead Books, 1995).

46 David James Duncan, *God Laughs and Plays* (Great Barrington, MA: Triad Books, 2006).

47 Eric Carmen, "All By Myself," *Eric Carmen* (1975).

48 Phil Collins, "Against All Odds," *Against All Odds* (1983).

49 Sir Mix-A-Lot, "Baby Got Back," *Mack Daddy* (1992).

50 Henri. J. M. Nouwen, *The Return of the Prodigal Son* (New York: Doubleday, 1994).

51 Henri Nouwen, *The Essential Henri Nouwen*, edited by Robert A. Jonas (Boston: Shambhala Publications, 2009).

52 Christine A. Colon and Bonnie E. Field, *Singled Out: Why Celibacy Must be Reinvented In Today's Church* (Grand Rapids, MI: Bra¬zo Press, 2009).

53 From Mother Teresa's essay for the Architects of Peace Project, which can be found at http://www.scu.edu/ethics/architects-of-peace/Teresa/lesson.html.

54 Shane Claiborne, *The Irresistible Revolution: Living as an Ordinary Radical* (Grand Rapids: Zondervan, 2006).

55 Frederick Buechner, *Now and Then: A Memoir of Vocation* (New York: HarperCollins, 1983). Emphasis mine.

56 David Janzen, *The Intentional Christian Community Handbook* (Brewster, MA: Paraclete Press, 2013). This is an excellent resource if you want to learn more about living in Christian community as I talk about it in this chapter.

57 Gene Edwards, *The Divine Romance* (Wheaton, IL: Tyndall House, 1992).

58 Kate Hurley, "Mary's Song," not yet recorded.

59 Henri Nouwen, *Seeds of Hope*, edited by Robert Durback (New York: Doubleday, 1997).

60 Selections from Gene Edwards, *The Divine Romance* (Wheaton, IL: Tyndall House, 1992), 227-229.

About the Author

Kate Hurley is a native of Colorado, where she resides in Boulder. The mission statement of her life *is to paint an accurate picture of a passionate God.* She has been a touring singer songwriter and worship leader for the last ten years. She also leads women's retreats and gatherings of worship leaders, and she teaches larger group gatherings as well. She has been a guest songwriter and musician for the acclaimed *Enter The Worship Circle* series and has made four solo CDs. She is passionate about loving the poor, and she tries to incorporate that into her work as much as possible. She loves food so much that she has been known to cry during a good meal.

You can listen to Kate's music on iTunes or on her website, www.katehurley.com, where you can also contact her for house shows, guest worship leading, speaking engagements, or freelance writing.

wonderful counselor   Almighty GOD   Elizabeth - blameless

* Make room → watch & wait
          *   * long for people
                      who long for me
Dec 10 7 ywam   enrolled with
            treasure   me, do not
            Hunts   get off
                              elevator @
                              ministry
Rest in
who He is
              Prince of
              peace   - wait & watch
Abba
Father
Everlasting   Show us what to let go
                  of so we can
                      watch & wait

lamps burning,
waists girded

CPSIA information can be obtained at www.ICGtesting.com
Printed in the USA
LVOW13s1958060913

351160LV00005B/15/P

consecrate the eyes of our heart